The Uffizi Gallery

The Top 30 Paintings to Visit
In Florence's Greatest Art Museum

Samuel Hilt, Ph.D.

A Tuscany Tours Book

TUSCANY TOURS

www.TuscanyTours.com

“Sam Hilt has written a book that I’ve been wanting for years: an intelligent, friendly guide to Italian art that makes the paintings come alive and connect to the life of the art lover. He quickly passes through the usual historical and technical aspects to help a viewer see and appreciate the images. So simple, and yet so radical. Sam is a person you would want at your side in an art museum, and his book is almost as good as him being there with you… Sam’s book reveals the heart and soul of the art. Its tone is just right—informative and insightful.”

Thomas Moore, New York Times’

Best-selling Author of *Care of the Soul*

(Contact info may be found on the succeeding page).

A Tuscany Tours Book

TUSCANY TOURS

www.TuscanyTours.com

Introduction

This guide has been developed to accompany you as you walk through the corridors of the Uffizi Museum looking at the strange and marvelous paintings that are collected here. Although the Uffizi is not nearly as huge and overwhelming as the Louvre in Paris or the Met in New York, there's still much more here than you can possibly absorb in the course of a visit. So, the strategy here has been to carefully pick out a few dozen paintings—out of the many hundreds—in whose company you will find it interesting and enjoyable to spend some time. It's still probably too much for a single visit, but if you sit down whenever you have the chance, and stop a couple of times for coffee breaks, it's almost possible.

The selection is based partly on the inherent interest of the paintings themselves, and partly on how well they are displayed. It's sad, but true, that certain paintings in the Uffizi are better seen in an art book than in their darkened rooms or where poorly positioned lighting reflects off the thick, bullet-proof glass. So, all of the paintings you will find included in this guide are not just "important", but are also displayed in the museum in a way that makes it possible to enjoy them.

The discussion of the paintings themselves is quite different than what you will find in most art history texts. My goal has been to help make these paintings come alive for you, and to make the experience of visiting them interesting, stimulating and memorable. Art guides often seem to focus intently on elements that are deadly boring to a general audience, and most of us have very little interest in the usual discussions about when a painting entered the museum's collection, whom it belonged to before that, whether it was painted exclusively by the Master himself or shows signs of intervention by his assistants, which scholars believe it was painted in 1458 and which ones argue for a dating of 1463, and so forth.

These kinds of discussions reflect the legitimate concern of art historians and belong in professional journals. Unfortunately, they do little to enhance our enjoyment when looking at paintings. The usual commentaries take our attention everywhere—except deeper into an encounter with the painting itself.

The discussions of the paintings that you will find in this guide try to stay as close as possible to the images themselves. However, since Italian Renaissance art is centuries distant and its religious and mythological themes are now unfamiliar to many of us, brief excursions into history or theology are sometimes essential to establish a meaningful context in which the images can be appreciated. Sacred themes are treated not as archeological relics, but as opportunities for spiritual reflection and insight in present terms. Occasionally, you will find suggestions for exercises that I've found helpful in working with a particular painting.

I hope you find this guide useful as you make your way through the amazing worlds of imagination that are housed in the Uffizi. I would enjoy hearing your thoughts and comments.

Sam Hilt
Siena, Italy
December, 2012
sam@tuscanytours.com

Table of Contents

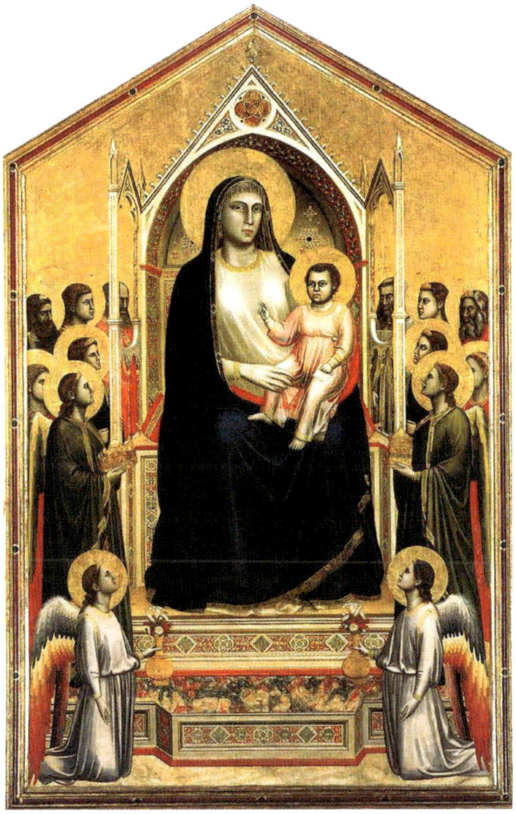

Figure 1: Giotto's *Ognissanti Madonna*

After you climb up the monumental stairs and arrive out of breath on the top floor of the Uffizi museum, turn left; the first room you can enter, Room 2, is off to your left. As you walk in you'll see an enormous painting of the Madonna and Child Enthroned in front of you. It's no accident that this painting is the first image presented for you to see. Known as the *Ognissanti Madonna*, it was painted in about 1310 by Giotto, who was considered the father of Florentine Renaissance art by many of the great artists who followed in his wake. And this particular image is often cited as an early instance of the new mode of painting that would flower during the Renaissance in the following century.

As you face Giotto's Madonna, off to your left is the Sienese artist Duccio's effort in the same genre, done about twenty years earlier, and on your right is Cimabue's treatment of the theme, done perhaps a decade before Duccio's. Each of these paintings once served as an altarpiece in a church for which it was commissioned. Since the altar occupies that special place in the church where contact between heaven and earth hopefully occurs, such altarpieces typically depicted sacred scenes, set in heaven, for the worshippers to contemplate. These are paintings that invite their viewers to direct their thoughts and energies heavenward.

While Cimabue's Madonna helped to define the conventions and possibilities of this genre, the images created by Duccio and Giotto take things further and are definitely more interesting. If you spend some time exploring the differences between these two paintings, you will begin to get a sense of the essential difference between Sienese and Florentine art. And, in that difference, you can experience the radical shift from a medieval relationship to the sacred which Duccio celebrates to the proto-Renaissance vision which Giotto helps to define.

As an experiment, spend a few minutes quietly in front of Duccio's Madonna. Imagine yourself in her presence. Make an effort to connect with her emotionally. You might try to engage her in imaginary conversation. Or, you might silently pose a question, and wait for a response.

Then, when you are ready, make your way across the room to Giotto's Madonna and repeat the experiment. How is it different?

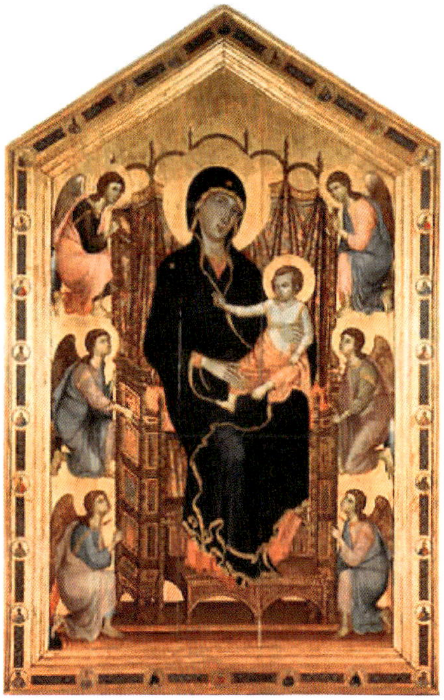

Figure 2: Duccio's *Rucellai Madonna*

Briefly, here's what happens for me: Duccio's Madonna is harder to get in touch with. For the image to "come alive" for me, I need to quiet my inner chit-chat and to probe psychically, intuitively, until a certain channel opens through which I experience a sense of connection and intimacy.

By contrast, when I stand before Giotto's Madonna, it feels like she is waiting to greet me. There is nothing elusive about her presence. A pretty, buxom young mother with rosy cheeks—who could be one of us—has suddenly come to dwell in our midst.

***

If you ever take an art history class or consult any guidebook about Renaissance art, you would find that Giotto's *Ognissanti* painting of the Madonna and Child is always celebrated as an important early use of perspective and as a milestone in the evolution of Western art. It's typically treated as an "advance" over Duccio's work because Giotto's figures appear to have physical mass and weight, and the painting shows considerable skill in the use of perspective to create spatial depth. But this is much the same as saying that the movie version of *Troy* starring Brad Pitt is a great advance over Homer's telling of the tale. After all, the movie actually shows us the battles and the blood spurting, whereas in the book we have to imagine them.

It's unfortunate that the appreciation of Giotto's achievement in creating "lifelike" figures always seems to go hand-in-hand with a disdain for the older sacred style which painted ethereal spirits as if they were just spirits and heavenly scenes as if they were not happening here on earth. A Madonna of weight and mass and realistic features is certainly innovative, but is not necessarily an "improvement" in any meaningful sense. Angels that stand on the ground and have weight and occupy space are not necessarily better suited for life in heaven, nor more able to help us imagine it, than their lighter brethren.

Throughout the Renaissance, Sienese art maintains a distinctive separation of the sacred and the everyday worlds. The figures continue to have a stylized beauty that prevents them from ever looking like our neighbors. Surfaces are ornate and flat, colors are marvelous, and perspective appears as a decorative element, rather than as a defining framework.

Although Duccio and Giotto try to invoke the presence of the Madonna through their arts, they go about it in distinctly different ways. Giotto's Madonna comes down to meet us at least half-way; Duccio's Madonna remains wholly an inhabitant of the higher realms.

To be able to appreciate Duccio's painting (and the thousands of other images that continue to be painted in this style over the next few centuries), we need to remind ourselves that these images were meant to portray sacred figures as they are in heaven. Duccio's angels appear to be floating around the Madonna's throne, light as feathers, kneeling on air itself. The Madonna herself sits so lightly on the throne that she appears almost weightless. The darkness of her robe set against the bright warm tones of the background brings her forward, and makes her appear to hover on the very surface of the painting, suspended in front of us.

To be able to appreciate Giotto's achievement, put aside the idea that he had any particular interest in advancing the art of "spacemaking" in pictorial representation. Art historical studies were still centuries away, and he was definitely not concerned with earning a place for himself in art survey courses. Instead, his intent would have been the same as other contemporary artists—to create powerful images that would enhance the experience of worship and the efficacy of prayer.

What's remarkable about Giotto's image is the *effect* of his spacemaking and of his use of mass and weight, not the mere fact of it. Mary's stature, mass, and realistic features serve to create the powerful impression of her physical presence in the room. And the newly created space behind her on the throne, like the angels who recede into the background alongside the throne, serve *to push the Madonna into the foreground, forward and into our space*. That's what Giotto is looking for; and pictorial depth was only a means toward that end.

He brings the faces of Mary and Jesus closer to us by painting their golden haloes directly on the surface of the picture plane. This sense of forward thrusting is also enhanced by the ways in which the flat, foreground haloes eclipse the background decorations of the throne. Finally, you can also confirm that this is a central intention of the painting by looking at the steps that lead up to the Madonna's throne. Look again and you'll realize that they are not really steps! The three "steps" are just decorative trim around the base of the platform on which the Madonna is seated. Why didn't Giotto use real steps? Because the recession of the steps would have pushed the Madonna on her throne further back into the picture plane. And this would have undermined the iconic effect that Giotto was seeking in bringing her as close to us as he could.

It's a gross misreading of this painting to focus obsessively on the spatial recession that Giotto created as if this were the point of the picture. Yet, it's a curious fact that those who are academically trained often seem to miss the powerful impact of the Madonna's presence and, instead, spend their time marveling at the emptiness behind her.

Simone Martini's *Annunciation* Room 3

Continuing to your left through Room 3, you'll see various 14th century Sienese paintings. Certainly the most beautiful of them is the *Annunciation* by Simone Martini, painted in 1333 for a chapel altar in the Cathedral of Siena.

Like most images of the Annunciation, the angel enters on the left and the Madonna is seated on the right. Often a column or pillar separates them, but in this scene, there's a vase filled with lilies. The words that the angel speaks, embossed in raised letters of gold, pass from his lips to her ear (*Ave Gratia Plenum* –"Hail, [Mary], full of grace"). The angel wears an olive wreath and holds out an olive branch in greeting, and as a peace offering. It invites us to recall the olive branch that the dove carried back to Noah signifying the end of the flood and the restoration of God's peace. The olive branch in this context suggests that the Annunciation reverses the Fall: it offers humanity new hope of redemption following our collective exile from Eden. Medieval theologians delighted in the significant coincidence that the angel's first word of greeting to Mary, *AVE*, is exactly the reverse spelling of *EVA*, the girl who ate the apple.

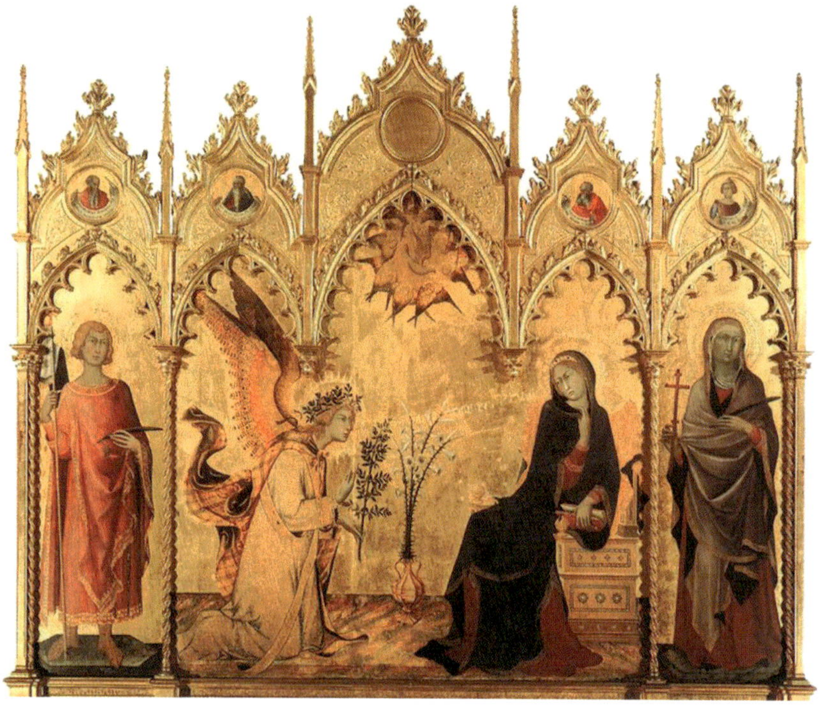

Figure 3: Simone Martini's *Annunciation*

Medieval sermons carefully distinguished between the different phases of the Virgin's response to the angel's visit. Briefly, we find an initial period of concern, alarm: "Who are you and what are you saying?" Then, incredulity and questioning: "How can this possibly come to be when I've never even been with a man?" Finally, understanding and acceptance: "Behold the servant of the Lord."

Different artists chose to represent different moments of the story ranging from initial shock to blissful acquiescence. One of the pleasures of looking at paintings of the Annunciation lies in identifying the moment of the story that the artist has chosen to illustrate, then observing how various elements of the painting support or dramatize the chosen moment.

As you look at Simone Martini's *Annunciation*, take a few moments and ask yourself where we are in the arc of the story: initial distress or blissful acceptance? Next, look carefully at the painting and see what details support your reading of the image. If you've brought pen and paper with you, you might want to jot them down.

***

My own sense of the story shown here is that we are at the very first moment of the angel's appearance. His plaid cloak is still fluttering (having just flown in from Scotland!). Mary clutches her robe closed tightly about her neck; the corners of her mouth are downturned. The words which the angel speaks are those with which the story begins. While the angel leans in from the left toward the center of the painting, Mary's body curves away from the center in an elegant, sweeping retreat.

In the vase which stands between the angel and Mary, the stems of the lilies appear to be covered with large, prickly thorns. And the dove, through whom the Incarnation will be miraculously achieved, still waits overhead, hovering, but held in check by a cordon of cherubs until the Virgin's consent can be obtained.

The words which Gabriel will later speak after Mary accepts her new role are already present, but are still curled up on the gold ribbon which streams around his shoulder and across the front of his gown. If you catch the light just right you can see the lettering on the streamer as well as Gabriel's name embossed on his sleeve.

Although Mary eventually agrees to play her role in the great drama of salvation, the fact that she could have chosen to do otherwise is an essential part of the Christian story. In that prior coupling of woman and bird that inaugurated the age of the Mycenaean Greeks, choice was absent. As the poet, Nils Peterson, expressed it:

> Here's all history:
> Leda could not say, "No";
> Mary could.

Gentile da Fabriano's *Adoration of the Magi* is certainly one of loveliest works of art created in fifteenth century Florence, and its exquisite beauty is even more apparent following its meticulous restoration in 2004. Yet it typically gets only meager praise because art historians are disturbed by the ways in which it blends the older sacred style with the newer naturalistic style. Instead of admiring Gentile's brilliant synthesis of both styles in creating a masterpiece, they praise what's "modern" about his work but complain about the continuing presence of "archaic" elements like golden skies and stylized figures. More about this later...

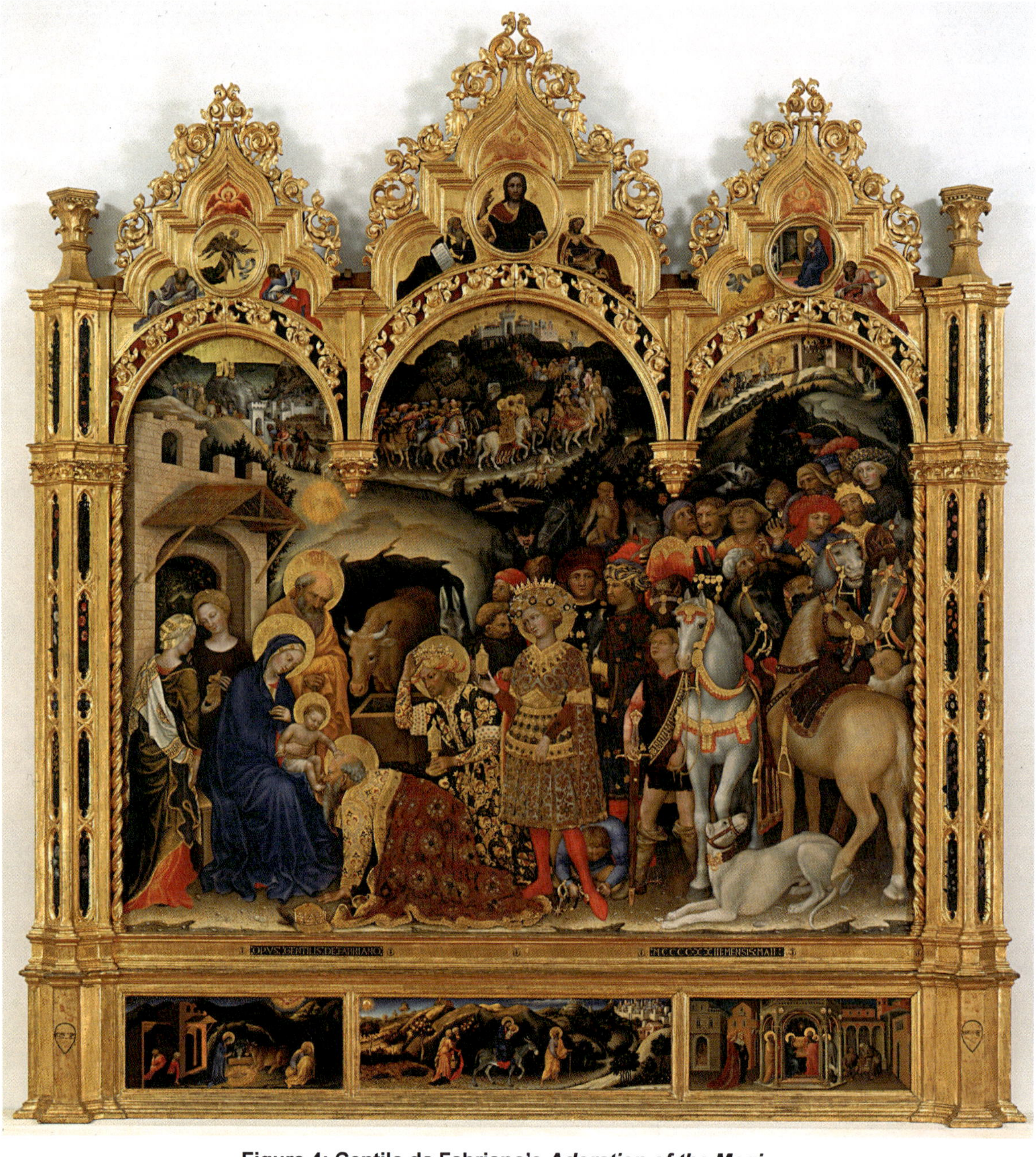

Figure 4: Gentile da Fabriano's *Adoration of the Magi*

The key event illustrated in this painting is based on the visit of the Magi to honor and brings gifts to the newborn Christ Child as described in the Gospel of Matthew. You can follow the story as it proceeds from top left to top right across the gables before bringing us down to the central event in the foreground below. In the gable on the top left, if you look carefully, you can see the Magi at the beginning of their journey—three tiny figures on a mountaintop surrounded by the brilliant sheen of hammered gold. From here they begin their descent into our world. In the central gable we see their procession approaching Jerusalem where they will meet with Herod, and in the rightmost arch we see them about to enter the town of Bethlehem where they will present their gifts to the infant Christ.

Very little of the detail we see is found in the Gospel narrative which is the ultimate source for this genre of painting. In the Gospel story the Magi are never identified as kings, nor is it stated how many of them there are. There is no mention of their respective ages; yet, by the time of the Renaissance, they come to be represented regularly as a youth, a man of middle age, and a balding elder. There is no mention of their national origins; yet, in later treatments, they are often shown to be of different races. (For example, have a look later at Albrecht Durer's *Adoration* located in Room 20, or Andrea Mantegna's in Room 23.)

Once you start looking carefully at the picture, you'll begin to notice all sorts of other elements that are not part of the Biblical story. If you brought your binoculars, this is a good time to pull them out. In the leftmost gable, as the Magi stand on the mountaintop looking at the star in the distance, someone is being mugged in the foreground below! In the central gable, over in the right foreground in front of the Magi, a deer has been brought down and another flees. A leopard crouches on the back of a horse about to spring. A hunting dog has also caught sight of the fleeing deer, and we are left to imagine the sequel. Behind the Magi, one horse has kicked another in the chest and retribution appears immanent. Meanwhile, the three kings, set slightly apart from the crowd behind and before them, ride on, unperturbed.

In the central foreground image, in the entourage surrounding the Magi and the Holy Family, Gentile shows us the mirth and frivolity of the common people, the raw vitality of their gestures and expressions. Here we find also an amazing and entirely implausible profusion of animal life: monkeys, greyhounds, leopards, camels, hawks swooping in mid-air. And in the center of this flurry of struggling horses, copulating birds, grinning peasants, jostling crowds, bursting pomegranates, and chained monkeys, we find the solemn, still figures of the Magi, crowned with gold, prostrating themselves before a baby born in a manger.

Notice how gold is used symbolically throughout the painting. The three gables that physically constitute the upper portion of the painting may be taken to represent the heavenly realms, the higher world, the ultimate source of gold. The journey of the Magi is an arc of descent, one which passes through our chaotic, dangerous world while beginning and ending on the mountaintops of gold. In the haloes and costumes of the sacred personages and in the gleam of the golden gifts that the Magi bring, we witness an event that results in the dispersion of gold from the upper reaches of sky to the world below.

The dramatic moment that Gentile emphasizes is the act of the eldest of the Magi kneeling and kissing the foot of the child, a gesture of the utmost abasement. The actions of the three Magi are orchestrated almost as if they were three phases of a single descending movement: the youngest king stands erect, his crown still in place; the middle king commences to kneel as he begins to remove his crown; the eldest stoops low, his crown beside him as the Christ Child blesses his bald pate. The Magi deign to pay homage to the golden haloed child who has appeared in a small village, born in a barn amidst the animals. That which is noblest and most regal prostrates itself before that which is most lowly, most helpless. The high makes itself low and sublimity descends to earth—thus the marriage of heaven and earth is consummated.

[If the notion of recurring archetypes is meaningful to you, you might pause to consider where, in our own times, this journey of the wise finds expression. For me, the three Magi who renounced privilege to make this same journey, and passed their light from one to the next, are Tolstoy, Gandhi, and Martin Luther King.]

***

Gentile da Fabriano was one of the earliest Renaissance artists to explore the subtleties of shadows, as in the *Adoration* scene on the far left of the predella (beneath the main painting) where the shepherds are illuminated by the angel's light, and also in the lovely central predella panel where light and shadow contour the hills. Yet, isn't it curious that the three Magi who present their gifts are depicted entirely without shadowing? Notice also the way that many of the figures in the painting are clearly set into the background landscape and modeled in the round. Yet the Magi are presented in the flat, patterned manner that was traditionally used in altarpieces to represent sacred personages.

Most art historians have responded to this blending of styles as an unfortunate occurrence, as if Gentile were a promising proto-modern artist who, alas, periodically succumbed to uncontrollable regressive tendencies. Yet, since Gentile is clearly quite skilled in using both the older sacred style as well as the newer naturalistic techniques, wouldn't it be more reasonable to assume that the mixture of styles in this image is deliberate?

Here's what I think he was up to: Look at the figures of the Magi, and you'll see how they seem to "float" on the surface of the picture plane. By using the sacred style of representation to depict them, Gentile pulls them forward while various other figures remain deeply immersed in the landscapes. This ingenious stroke enables Gentile to depict the three Magi as beings "who are in this world, but not of it". And, indeed, the exquisite contrast between these otherworldly beings and the motley world of humanity through which they journey is at the heart of the painting's visual interest and also the source of its deepest significance.

Continuing on to Room 5, you can't miss the large, lavish altarpiece by Lorenzo Monaco depicting the Coronation of the Virgin. "Monaco" means monk, and Lorenzo belonged to the Camaldolese order in Florence. He painted tiny miniatures in illuminated manuscripts, massive altarpieces, and everything in between. Much of his work has the same lovely, lyrical quality that's shown in this Coronation altarpiece, done in 1413.

Coronations are particularly difficult for a modern audience to appreciate since there doesn't seem to be much "happening." They are contemplative images, rather than narrative or dramatic episodes. For starters, you might find it helpful to think of the Coronation as the final epiphany in the story, just as the Annunciation (shown on the pinnacle panels above) is the initial moment that sets the story in motion.

The Coronation of the Virgin occurs after Mary's Assumption into heaven, and it portrays the moment in which she is crowned as Queen of Heaven. In medieval Christianity the Coronation of the Virgin is the end of the story, its *telos*, that end toward which everything proceeds. Whereas modern Christianity tends to keep the image of Christ Crucified foremost in our minds, earlier worship treated the Crucifixion somewhat differently. It was depicted as the critical moment in a story that then continues beyond it and culminates in the death of the Virgin, her Assumption into heaven, and her ultimate Coronation. It is the Coronation image that one often finds in the pinnacle of the facade of churches and cathedrals, and in the frescoes over their high altars. For several centuries in popular worship and pictorial representation, if not in orthodox theology, Mary occupied this most elevated place—before being dethroned and demoted in the post-Reformation era to the status of surrogate mother.

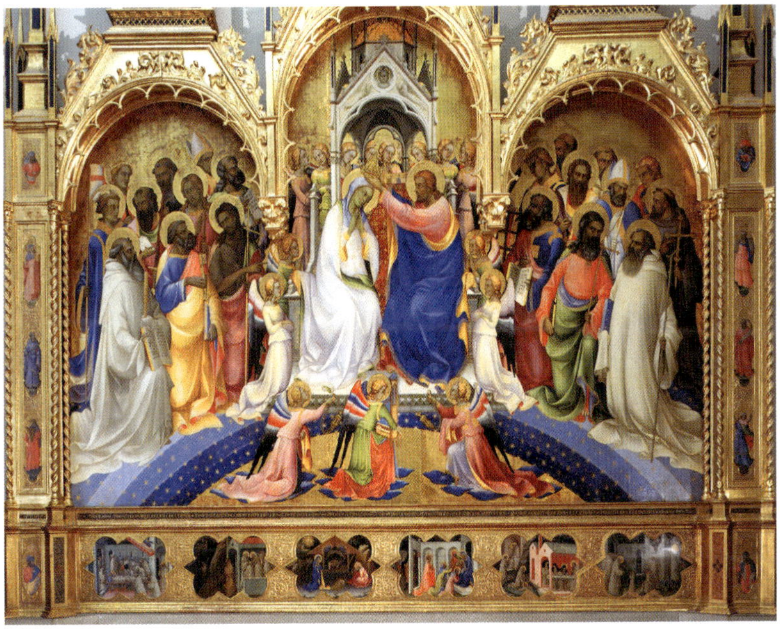

Figure 5: Lorenzo Monaco's *Coronation*

(It's interesting to note that it was not until November 1, 1950, that Mary's Assumption into heaven was finally proclaimed as Catholic dogma and became a part of orthodox belief!)

Because of its exalted topic, paintings of the Coronation, like this one by Lorenzo Monaco, are often lavish, colorful and extravagant. Whenever they depict this theme, artists are challenged to pull out all the stops as they try to portray the heavenly court celebrating this most joyous event. Lorenzo shows us seven starry bands in the foreground beneath the feet of Christ and the Virgin. These bands represent the planetary spheres, and they indicate that the event we see is taking place beyond them, in the highest heaven.

The ritual of Coronation, carried out before all the heavenly host, confirms Mary in her new role as Queen of Heaven. It's the moment when the angels blow their trumpets, and Mary, and all she represents, are given their due. In certain images of the Coronation, like the mosaics in the church of Santa Maria Maggiore in Rome, Mary is shown with the moon beneath her feet, as Christ is shown with the sun beneath his. There's a suggestion in these images of Coronation of a mystical marriage, a *conjunctio*, and of the sacred feminine taking its honored place in heaven. And, just as the Annunciation in the gables above shows us the beginning of Mary's story, the Coronation portrays its final act.

One way to enjoy such images is to imagine that you've been invited to this celebration and to simply let yourself delight in the delicate colors, the elegance and the pageantry. I sometimes think of the ladder of being that extends from God through the angels to the saints down to us. When we participate imaginatively in these images, we become honorary members of the congregation. And I remind myself that although we stand on the lowest rung, we are, after all, the ones who make these pictures.

While you're thinking about Coronations, walk over to Room 7 and look at Fra Angelico's treatment of the same theme. In Italy, Fra Angelico has long been known as "Beato Angelico," and he was, in fact, beatified by the Church in 1983. It's not impossible that he may someday come to be known as "Saint Angelico".

His panel is much smaller than Lorenzo's, yet it has a remarkable intensity. Angels blow trumpets, play stringed instruments and swing censers. The flood of golden light behind Christ and the Virgin is almost like an explosion or a sunrise, and it suggests that we are witnessing the visible portion of an ineffable event too great for the eye to see. In the foreground on the right we can see Mary Magdalen kneeling. She wears a red dress and holds a golden jar. She is turned toward us, as if to acknowledge our presence, yet her expression and the directness of her gaze seem almost to challenge us. Now that you're here, do you have any idea what you're looking at, Mr. Jones?

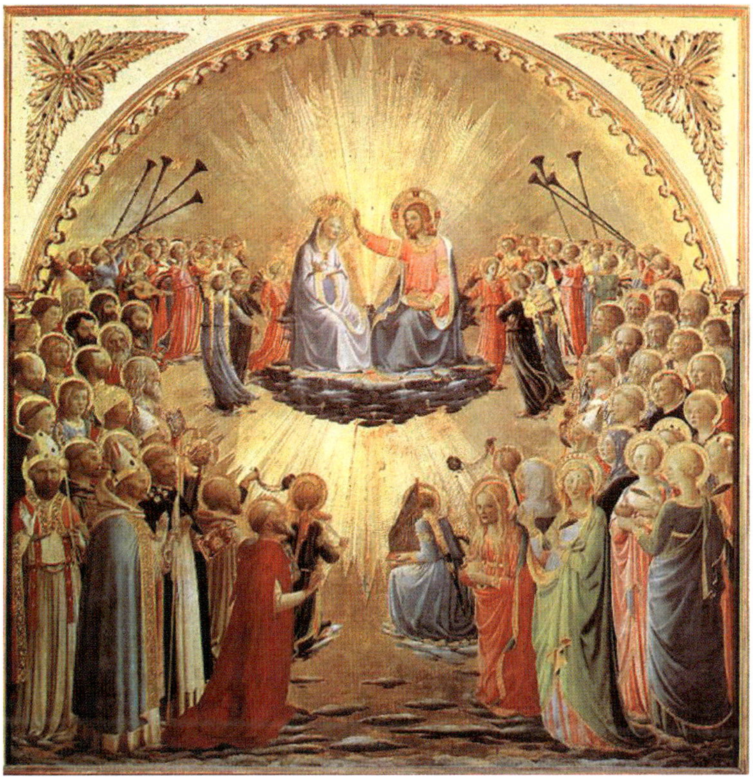

Figure 6: Fra Angelico's *Coronation*

If you look carefully at the assembled host, you'll see that they form a sort of circle at the center of which we find Christ and the Virgin. The various figures, along with Mary Magdalen, who look outwards toward us implicate us and our presence in the structure of the painting. We, as spectators, constitute an outer ring, further from the Inner Realms but not excluded from them. The parting of the circle before us, front and center, invites our imaginative participation in this celestial gathering.

There's a feeling in many of Fra Angelico's *Coronations* that they depict mystical events from the perspective of a participant, rather than a mere observer. Knowing what we do about the religious practices of the Monastery of San Marco where Fra Angelico spent his life, it's reasonable to assume that his own visionary experience is the secret ingredient that gives his paintings their special magic. If his Annunciation at the top of the stairs in San Marco shows Mary at the beginning of her spiritual journey, images like this one portray its triumphal culmination.

Although Fra Angelico's greatest painting of the Coronation is currently housed in the Louvre, this panel, along with his other Coronation images that can be seen at San Marco, show him to be the great master of this genre. In C.S. Lewis' phrase, he is "further up and further in" than many of his contemporaries who attempt to depict the same themes. After spending time immersed in Fra Angelico's dreamlike *Coronation*, going back to Lorenzo's, lovely as it is, feels a bit like going to a dress-up event that's mainly for show.

In the same room as Fra Angelico's *Coronation*, centrally located, are a small pair of beautifully framed panels painted by Piero della Francesca. The couple whose portraits you see, Federigo da Montefeltro and Battista Sforza, were rulers of the dukedom of Urbino in the latter half of the 15th century. Piero was resident in Urbino for some of this time and executed several commissioned works for them. This is one of the handful that survives.

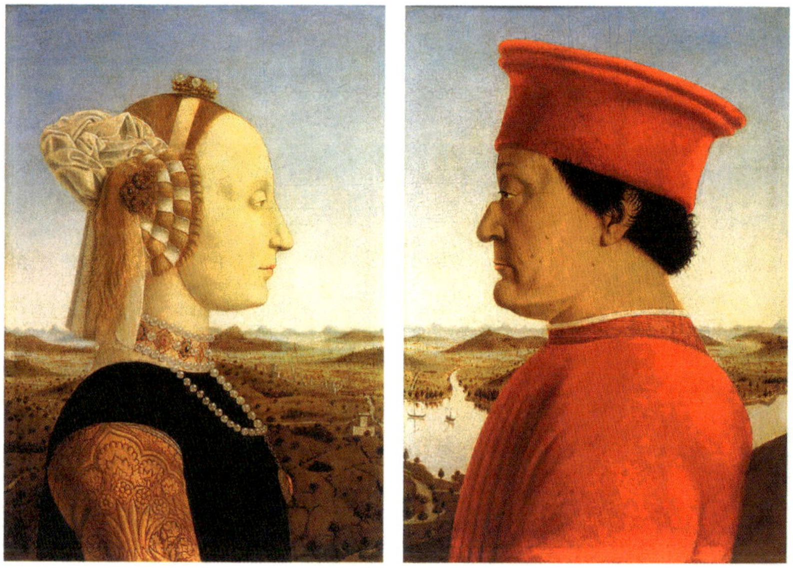

Figure 7: Piero della Francesca's *Duke and Duchess of Urbino*

Take a minute and look at the panels from both sides. On the reverse side of their portraits we see them riding on carriages in a triumphal procession. If you ignore the frame for a moment, you can see that the landscape in the background is actually continuous between the two panels on each side. Even though the panels are fairly small and the landscapes are already far in the distance, if you look carefully you'll see that everything in the landscape continues to diminish and recede in perfect perspective as the eye moves toward the horizon.

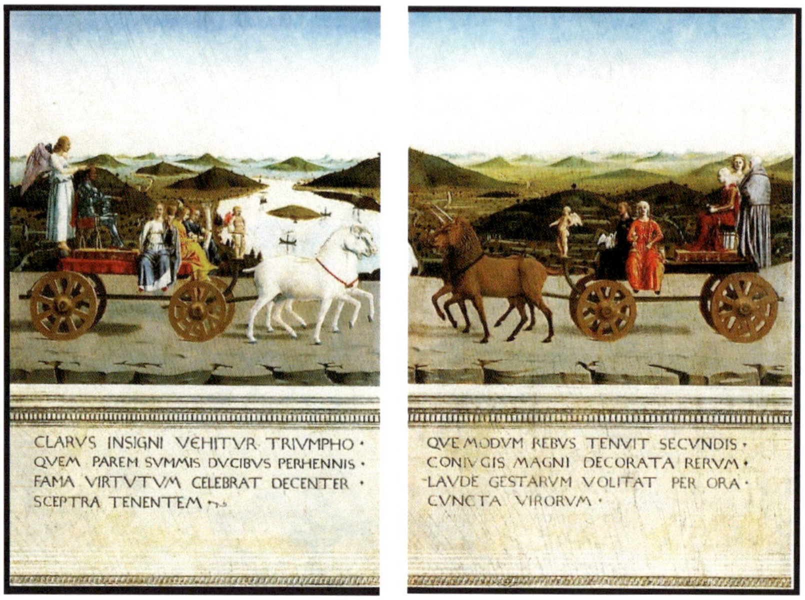

Piero's painting is an homage to this remarkable couple which celebrates both their relationship and their role in providing stewardship for their realm. If anyone tells you that the partnership model of relationship was a late 20th century feminist invention, just send them here for a look at similar ideals expressed five centuries earlier.

The carriage scenes on the back of the portraits are known as "Triumphs," and they can best be understood as exalted representations of certain qualities associated with the two rulers. The four figures who ride on Federigo's carriage represent what are known as the Cardinal Virtues. These have to do with qualities that impact a person's dealings with the world, attributes like sound judgment, courage, fairness and forbearance. The figures who ride with Battista represent the Theological Virtues, such as faith and compassion, which are important for the soul's development and well-being.

The contrast between these diverse, but complementary, orientations is developed further in the depiction of the activities of the Duke and Duchess on their respective carriages. Federigo looks straight ahead at the world, holding his scepter extended before him. Battista looks toward the book in her lap and is inwardly engaged. While Federigo's chariot is pulled by real horses, Battista's is pulled forward by unicorns. Pragmatic realism and visionary idealism come toward each other.

The perfect symmetry of the pictures suggests that neither party in this relationship is more, nor less, important than the other and implies a parity between them, both as rulers and as husband and wife. This is even reflected in the inscriptions beneath their Triumphs which are each three and one-half lines in length, and which praise their virtues in exactly the same number of words.

Come back again to the portraits and you'll see how these same themes are subtly developed in the portraits themselves. These portraits are typically praised for their "realism", but this really misses the point. Battista is actually shown in a highly idealized manner: her complexion is perfect and her skin is unnaturally pale; her hair is beautifully tressed and interlaced with intricately folded silk; her crown and neckline are ornamented with lustrous pearls and gems. Beside her, Federigo is shown with his broken nose, his hair growing over his ears, the crow's foot in the corner of his eye, even the moles on his cheek. The polarity between them is as palpable as their profound unity. They stand erect, their heads just above the distant horizon. Just as the panels are evenly divided between earth and sky, so do they hold together heaven and earth.

Before we leave them, there's one more thing to do. Take a moment and imagine that they are looking at each other. Do you see how they look at each other, seeing and allowing themselves to be seen? For better and for worse, as if eternally exchanging vows at a marriage: the king, the queen, and the land.

Fra Filippo Lippi **Room 8**

Room 8 is dedicated primarily to the work of Fra Filippo Lippi. Up to this point there's been very little discussion of artists' lives and personalities. Partly, this is because very little substantive information about the lives of the early Renaissance artists has come down to us. And, when we do reflect upon what we know about men like Brunelleschi, Donatello or Masaccio, there is little reason to assume that they used their art as a vehicle for personal expression.

When we approach Filippo Lippi, however, we're in a radically different situation. Filippo was definitely a "character." And, he was such a strong character that the imprint of his personality is everywhere present in his work.

Unlike Fra Angelico who was a holy soul and thrived within the confines of monastic life, Filippo Lippi was dragged kicking and screaming into a monastery after his father died and the relatives couldn't afford to keep him. It's hard to imagine someone less temperamentally suited for such a life. A famous anecdote about him concerns a commission he received to paint an altarpiece for the convent of Santa Margherita. He somehow managed to obtain permission from the Mother Superior to allow one of the nuns to sit as his model for the Virgin Mary. They wound up as lovers living "off campus," and she eventually bore him a son who would become the painter Filippino Lippi (whose work is exhibited across the room).

Whereas Giotto dared to imagine the Madonna as a woman of flesh and blood, Filippo carried the impetus of radical de-sublimation even further by proceeding to seduce her. Let's look at a couple of his paintings, bearing in mind that we are dealing with a black sheep in the house of God.

The *Coronation of the Virgin* here in Room 8 is one of two paintings that Lippi left us which contain unmistakable self-portraits (the other is the *Barbadori Altarpiece* in the Louvre). If you look toward the bottom left corner of the painting, there are two monks standing side-by-side. One is a grey-haired, grey-robed elder gazing reverently at the stage; the other is Filippo with his hand under his chin and his elbow casually propped up on the railing, looking right out at us.

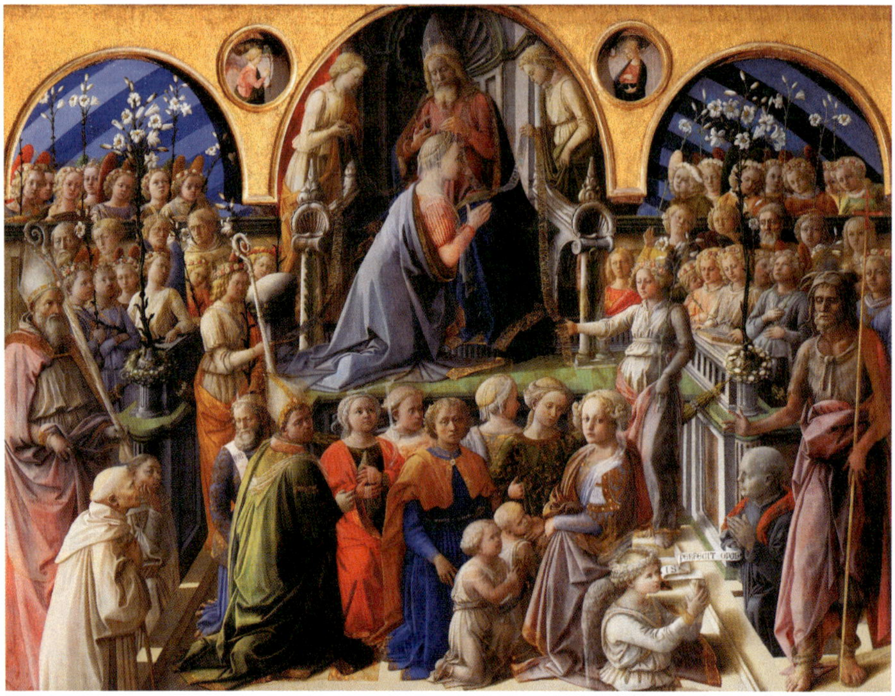

Figure 8: Fra Filippo Lippi's *Coronation of the Virgin*

Not only is Filippo not paying attention to the Coronation, neither are any of the angels. Their heads are turned every which way; they look up, down, sideways, only not at that which is supposed to be the object of their wholehearted devotion. As we scan the faces of the assembled angelic hosts of heaven, not a single one engages us with a look of beauty or intelligence or spiritual power. To anyone who has exchanged glances with the angels that inhabit the worlds depicted by Duccio, Fra Angelico or Piero della Francesca, the contrast is striking.

Fillipo's angels are slightly sleepy kids with vague, diffused looks. The most remarkable thing about them is their ordinariness.

Watch carefully where your attention actually goes as you spend some time in front of the *Coronation of the Virgin*, and you'll begin to notice some interesting things. Even though the Coronation is presumably the reason for the painting, and Christ and Mary are made larger than life, the ritual itself fails to hold our interest. The Virgin's slight turn away from us removes the possibility of representing any expressiveness of character, and the act of Coronation itself seems almost perfunctory.

What I believe you will discover, after a few moments in front of the painting, is that the figures which actually merit and capture our attention are those closest to us in the foreground. In particular, there is a lovely blonde in the right foreground shown with her two children and her husband, St. Eustace. Once we notice her looking out at us, it's hard to look at the picture without being drawn immediately to her face. And what an interesting face she has! When we compare her poise and her strongly delineated character with that of any of the angels, we see the difference between a woman who has lived and a gaggle of innocent children who seem to have tasted so little of life.

If we look more closely at her own children, it is interesting to note how little they resemble each other. The one on the left has the same hair and refined features as his father, while the one on the right doesn't look at all like him. Yet it's this child whose face she holds and caresses with her open palm while the other child extends his clasped hands and seems to plead for her attention. Is there an implicit preference for the one over the other? And doesn't the child whose face she presents to us resemble the kneeling figure on the left in the long green robe far more than it does the face of her husband? Interestingly enough, the tilt and angle of the child's face and the face of the man in the green robe are almost identical. How odd that these two should be the ones who look out at us directly, half turned toward us and half turned away--and with her husband directly between them.

Look at the strange way the child (whose face she touches) has grabbed his mother's fingers. He holds the ring finger and pinky of her left hand in such a way as to make his own hands look like little hoofs. Or, perhaps like little horns? Is there a suggestion here that St. Eustace—who beheld a vision of a great stag—may have a wife who's been unfaithful?

At some point we remember Filippo Lippi in the left foreground with his head in his hand, looking directly at us. His look says: "There's a Coronation going on, a sacred event, and somehow you've gotten caught up in fantasizing about the love life of the proud beauty with the young children. *O, hypocrite lecteur, mon semblable mon frere!" ("You there, you hypocrite, my brother, my twin," as Charles Baudelaire put it.)*

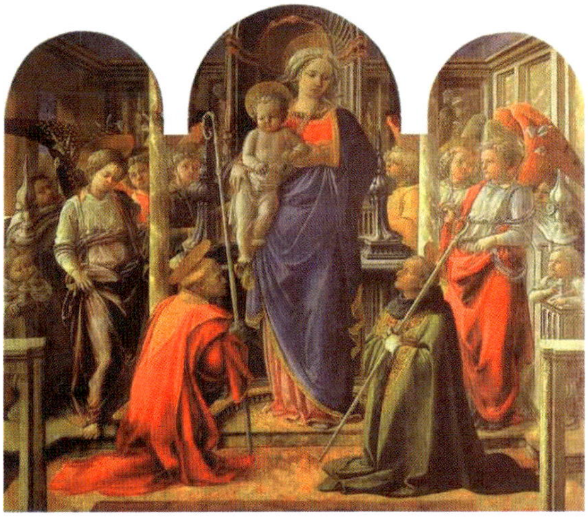

Figure 9: Lippi's *Barbadori Altarpiece*

Once you tune into this level of irony, humor and subterfuge in Filippo Lippi's work, it's fascinating to watch it play out in his paintings—and hilarious to read the deadpan, reverential commentaries on his work. In the painting mentioned earlier, the *Barbadori Altarpiece* that hangs in the Louvre (reproduced here as Figure 9), Filippo is once again the odd man out on the far left with his chin propped on the railing. The angels look up, down and all around, but not even one of them looks at the Madonna and Child. The angel at the front left stares intently at his bony right foot. Mary and the Babe look somewhat sad and apprehensive. The drama in the image seems to center on whether or not Mary will trip over the Bishop's miter as she steps off the dais. And, interestingly enough, every single figure in the painting has a touch of gold somewhere—except for our man Filippo! Certainly enough to make anyone suspicious, one would think, yet somehow it all sailed right past the patrons who commissioned the altarpiece, and the generations of critics who have praised the painting's religious splendor.

Walk over now to the painting known as *The Madonna and Child with Two Angels*. It's the painting with the curly-haired angel that looks at us with a big grin. The face of the Madonna is often reproduced by itself and sold in gift shops as an icon, an image of piety. But, look again, and you'll see why the angel is amused. Mary sits with her right shoulder against the very edge of the window frame. Her body, however, continues to extend right out the window. And the little angel whose face we see just beneath the Christ Child's arms can only be hanging out the window in mid-air.

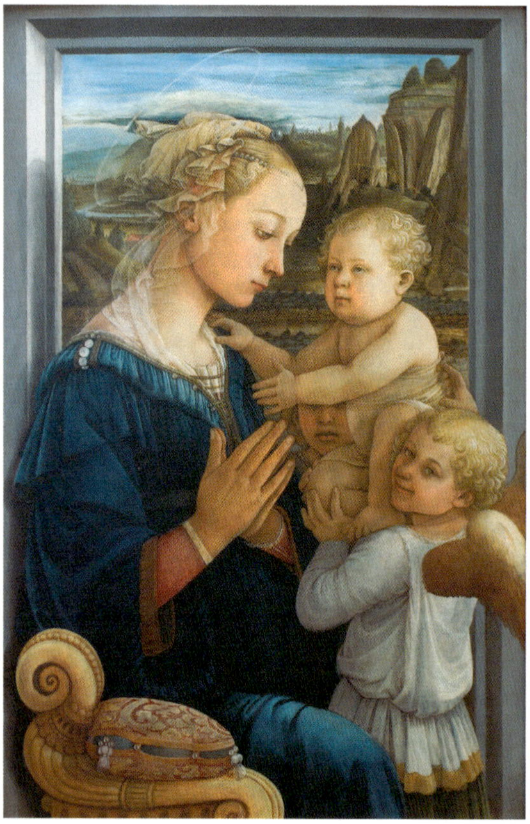

Figure 10: Lippi's *Madonna with Two Angels*

Equally odd, though less funny, is the manner in which the pious mother ignores everything around her. Even though two angels are holding her baby up in front of her as he looks for some attention, she's definitely off in her own world and is completely oblivious to the child.

There are many Renaissance artists who show us the most profound rapport and affection between Madonna and Bambino in one painting after another. Yet the more you look at Filippo's images of mother and child, the more you realize how dysfunctional his mothers always are and how solitary and unloved are their infants.

It's not until after Filippo's own child is born in his later years that we find him painting images of babies receiving abundant love from adoring mothers. In fact, Filippo invents from scratch an entirely new genre during this period of his life called *The Adoration of the Child*, two examples of which are displayed in this room on either side of his *Coronation*. These are somewhat similar to Nativity scenes, but with a significant difference: they show the mother directly adoring the child.

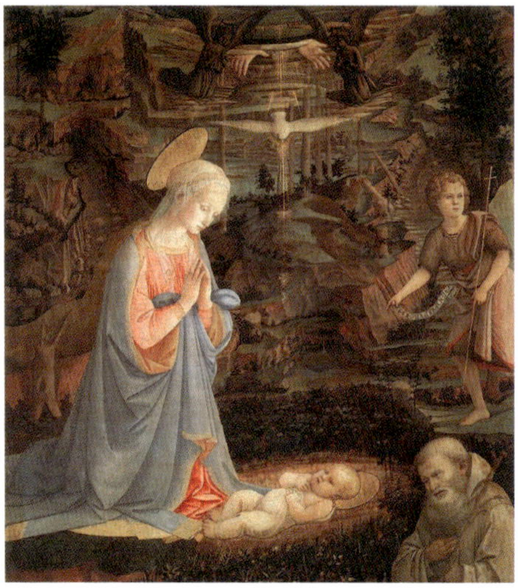

Figure 11: Lippi's *Adoration of the Child*

In these lyrical images of cuddly infants receiving their mother's direct attention (along with various saints and angels who come, as well, to pray for their well-being), we find images of the Christ Child which, for the first time, remind us of real infants.

In these Adoration images, I find none of that ironic edge that's present in so much of his other work. I do have my suspicions, however, that if we had any baby pictures of the little Filippino, they would bear a striking resemblance to the cute little babes we find here.

As you make your way from Filippo Lippi's work into the adjacent rooms that house Botticelli's masterpieces, it's worth noting that Filippo was Botticelli's teacher. And, after Filippo's death, it was Botticelli who took over the artistic education of Filippo's son, Filippino Lippi.

Although they languish under greenish-tinted bulletproof glass, Botticelli's *Birth of Venus* and his *Primavera* still retain much of their magic. These are mysterious, dream-like images that invite interpretation, and there is certainly no shortage of fascinating and conflicting readings. It's fun to speculate about their meanings, and totally appropriate, but let's begin with what we know that can provide some orientation.

One of the first things worth noting about these two paintings is that they were among the first large-size paintings during the Renaissance to depict mythological subjects. Mythological themes were common on decorative platters and household furnishings, but, before Botticelli, painting on this scale was reserved for altarpieces with Christian themes. Simply by working on this scale Botticelli invites us to treat these images with a degree of seriousness not usually devoted to mythological topics.

Another thing we know about these two paintings is that they were intended for the edification of the adolescent nephew of Lorenzo de' Medici, ruler of Florence. We know something, even today, about teenage boys and pictures of beautiful naked women, so we can be fairly sure that he was not unhappy with this gift. But we also know that Lorenzo was the patron of the Florentine Platonic academy and that he and his cousin, Lorenzo di Pierfrancesco, probably had a more complex agenda in mind when they commissioned the work from Botticelli.

Botticelli was an integral part of this circle of poets and scholars and artists who were deeply committed to recovering the esoteric wisdom of the ancient pagan world and integrating it with contemporary Christian belief. One member of the group, Marsilio Ficino, even wrote a book called *Platonic Theology* in which he tried to show that Plato's mystical teachings about the soul were entirely compatible with Christian dogma. So, it's in this context that we need to begin looking at the *Primavera* and the *Birth of Venus*.

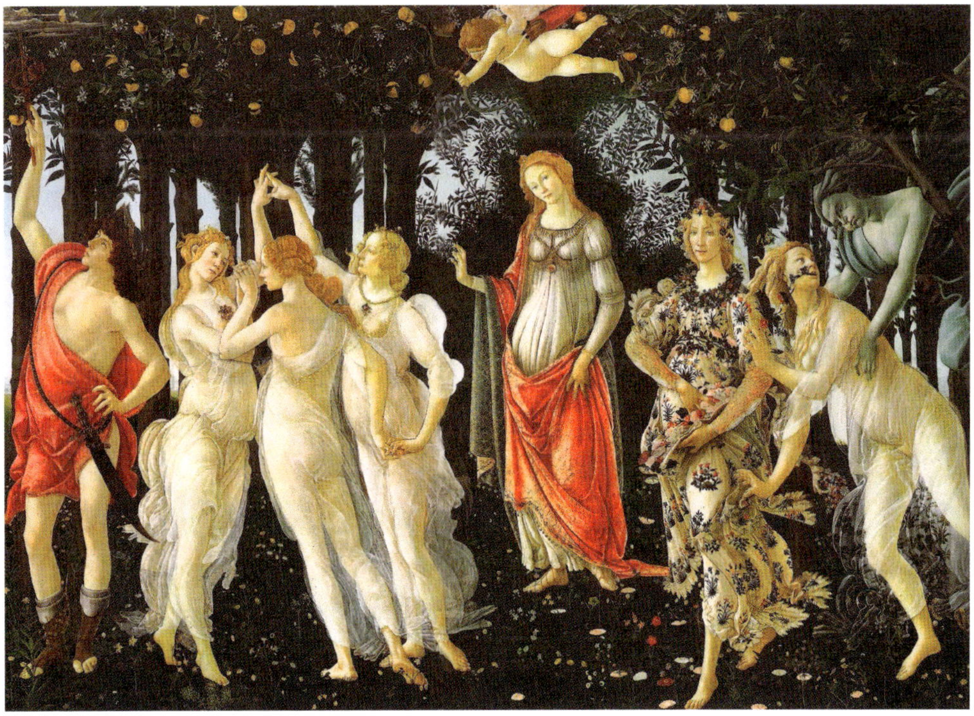

Figure 12: Botticelli's *Primavera*

Let's start with the *Primavera* (which was completed a few years before its companion piece). As we explore, we'll try to stay close to what we can actually observe without going too far afield into classical sources. First of all, if you step back and look at the movement within the image, you'll notice that things seem to move from right to left. Most of the figures in the painting are turned toward or facing our left; some are leaning that way; and blindfolded Cupid is aiming his arrow in that direction. So, the ways in which the figures are standing, looking and gesturing draw our attention across the canvas from right to left.

Now, notice also how our focus moves up and down as we move right to left. The winged blue figure descends from the heavens and bends the branches of the trees as he crashes through them. You can see his blue wing in the upper right corner of the painting. (This is, incidentally, the only area of the upper foliage that is barren of fruit.)

From him we pass down to the nymph he has grabbed, then, an upward diagonal carries our eye to the woman scattering flowers and on to the regal figure in the center of the painting. Her outstretched hand moves our eye down to the first of the dancing maidens, then up to the hand-bridge over the head of the middle dancer, down to the last and, finally, over to the young man who pulls our eyes upward as he pokes his wand into the clouds on the upper left.

The up-and-down dance that our eye performs as it moves across the painting perfectly mirrors the dance of the three maidens who raise and lower their joined hands as they circle. Isn't this an exquisite way of inviting us to join the festivities?

***

Now, let's look more closely at the figures in this dance as we make our way from right to left. The movement begins with the aerial creature who has come down from the heavens. He's blue—like the sky behind him, like our flesh in the cold of winter, like depression, like aching gonadal longing. His entrance on the scene seems to be abrupt, unexpected, somewhat frightening, at least for the nymph who leans away from him as if trying to flee. Yet, whatever it is that transpires between them brings forth a stream of flowers from her mouth.

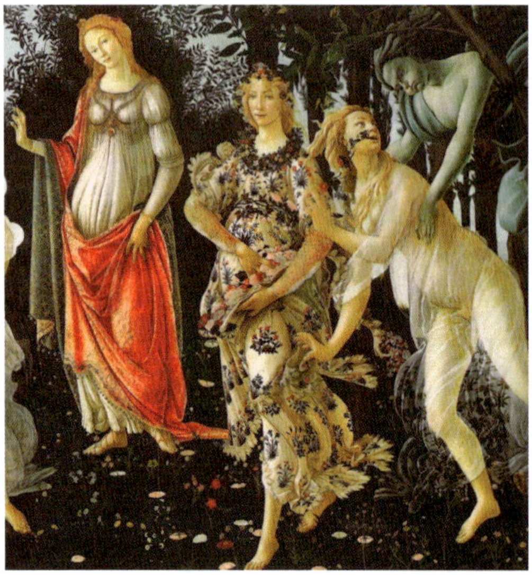

The figure to her left with the floral gown doesn't share in her apparent distress, but simply prepares to scatter a handful of the flowers which she has gathered in the fold of her dress. The green-leafed vine with pink flowers that emerges from the first girl's mouth merges with the flowers of the other girl's dress and appears again in the garland that she wears in her hair. Also, if you look closely at the nymph's hands, you'll see that there are places where the flowers of the dress grow over her hands and other places where they are visible through them. All of which—in this age before morphing technologies—suggests that the first girl precedes and is mysteriously transformed into the second.

In fact, when we look at the three female figures as an ascending series, we notice a variety of progressive changes:

- The first figure is virtually nude, wearing only a filmy gown. Her hair is loose and undressed. Her feet are bare.
- The second figure wears a flower dress and sports a floral necklace; her waist is girdled by a flowery vine (which, like the necklace, may be part of the dress). Her hair is loose, but dressed with a garland. Her feet are bare.

- The third figure is dressed in tailored clothes. Her robe of red and blue shows detailed workmanship in the fabric patterns and the decorative bordering along the hemline. She wears gold jewelry. Her hair is carefully braided, and she wears a jeweled headdress. Her feet are shod.
- The first figure tries to run away; the second walks purposefully; the third stands and presides.

The sequence invites us to think in terms of three aspects of the feminine or three stages in the life of woman: the alluring nymph, naked and unfettered; the fruitful, flowering young mother; the mature woman: poised, self-possessed, sophisticated.

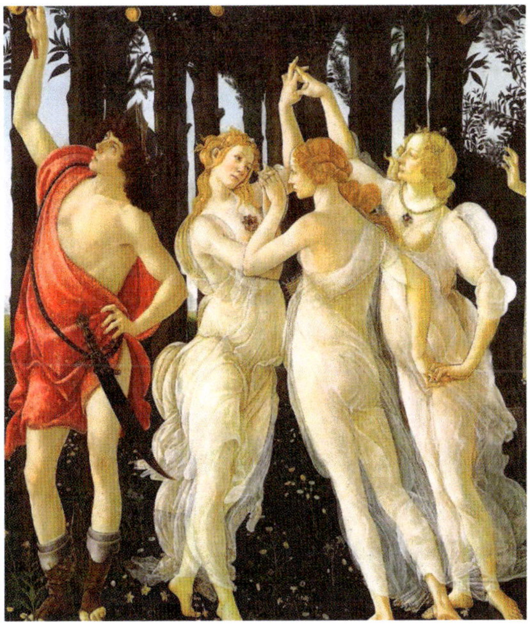

Scholars who believe they have found the mythological sources of these mysterious figures identify them as Zephyr, the wind god; Chloris, the nymph whom he pursues; Flora, the goddess of springtime and flowers; and Venus, the goddess of love and beauty. But one of the things that's marvelous about Botticelli's image is that we don't really need labels: the figures already show us who they are. In the ways that they move, dress and carry themselves, they embody the play of energies that reference to the classical myths merely confirms.

As we move left, the dance continues. Over the head of Venus/Aphrodite, a blindfolded Cupid gets ready to shoot a fiery-tipped arrow at one of the dancers (familiar to most of us as "The Three Graces"). If you carefully follow the line of the arrow, you'll discover its intended target. It's the middle dancer, the one whose shoulder is bare, her buttons all undone. The other two are holding their bridged hands over her head like a canopy. She stares intently at the young man off to her left who is poking around in the clouds. We're left to imagine, now that he's caught her eye, what will happen once the arrow strikes.

The young man on the far left is draped in an elegant fabric; his feet are shod and his sandals have wings. He carries a sword and wears a sort of helmet or crown. In his right hand he holds a caduceus, a wand around which two snakes intertwine. The caduceus is associated today with medicine and healing, but formerly would have been recognized as a sort of magic wand. Our young man is using his tool for exploring the mysteries of the heavens where his gaze and his attention are fixed. We're reminded of Aldous Huxley's definition of a genius as someone who doesn't think about sex all the time.

Note the perfect symmetry between the couples who frame the dance before us. We begin with an aerial creature who is pulled downward by hunger and desire while the nymph he grasps flourishes and flowers. And we end with a maiden about to fall in love with a young man of noble bearing whose thoughts are fixed on celestial things. If we think once again about the education of Lorenzo's nephew, we might imagine him learning about how love hits us wildly from below, then transforms us, and ultimately carries us to the threshold of sublimity. The male entering Aphrodite's realm dives in headlong but exits standing upright, marveling at the heavenly majesty of it all. The woman is startled and apprehensive at her initiation into the mysteries of the body, but she then moves gracefully through them and is ultimately lured beyond them.

Part of the inexhaustible fascination of the image is the sense of a world where all is as it should be; where art, beauty and love are in perfect harmony; where the dance of earthly desire is revealed in its correspondences to the cosmic cycle of renewal. In this pagan dream of the Renaissance, we stop to marvel at the sophisticated embrace of eros in all its differentiations from lust through graciousness. And it makes our own dominant conception of sex as an animal need or “instinctual drive” seem almost barbarous by comparison.

When we shift our attention to the *Birth of Venus*, we recognize certain elements from the *Primavera*: the winged figure with blue cape and puffed cheeks; the nymph with the wild, wavy blonde hair who now appears to be his mate; the profusion of pink flowers; a floral dress with flowering vine around the neck and the waist; the grove of trees. Things are similar, but somewhat different.

The winged figure and the nymph that clings to him are now in a very different phase of their relationship than the one we saw in the *Primavera*. He is no longer blue all over; his skin now has warm flesh tones. Given his line of work, his cheeks are still puffed, but his face has lost that desperate intensity. The relationship appears to have infused him with new vitality.

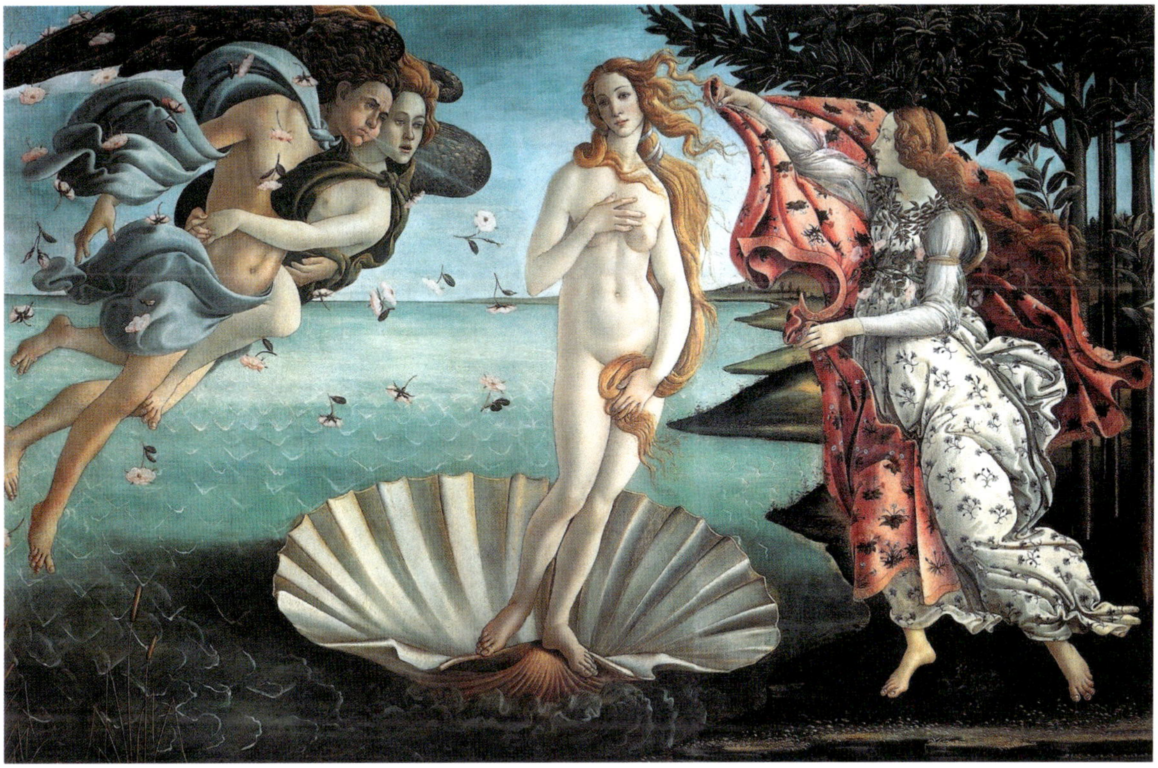

Figure 13: Botticelli's *Birth of Venus*

The nymph who leaned away from him apprehensively in the *Primavera* now trusts him enough to let him transport her through the air. She holds on to him like a young girl on the back of a motorcycle clinging tightly to her boyfriend and enjoying the ride.

Anyone can see that these two are now a couple. In fact, with her body wrapped all around him in the way that it is, they are so coupled that it's hard to tell whose legs are whose. If you look closely, you can see the breath stream coming out of her mouth as well as his. The energies of their coupling with its huffing and puffing and fluttering is providing the motive force that brings Venus ashore.

The couple on the left are bringing a host of pink flowers in their wake. It's almost as if traveling in a cloud of flowering pink blossoms were the "objective correlative", or external mirror, of their inner state of being. Meanwhile, the maiden on the right rushes forward to drape Aphrodite in an elegant pink floral cape. The flowers on this garment are woven and designed—as distinct from the "real" flowers brought by the couple on the left. Like the cape itself with its elegantly embroidered hem, these flowers are a product of art, rather than of nature.

All of this suggests that Aphrodite is fed by nature on one side and culture on the other, and that she is, herself, the matrix in which they are united. Like her hair which runs from head to loins, her gesture and stance echo this union of higher and lower. One foot stands flat and honors gravity, the other lifts up and suggests ascent. And, after we lift our eyes above her breasts, we may notice that her right hand is gently placed over her heart while she holds her left hand over her pubis, and seems to reflect on the mysterious relationship between these two domains.

***

You may remember that Venus is born from the severed genitals of Uranus after they are tossed into the sea. This is a very difficult image for us to connect with the loveliness of the goddess. But this aspect of the myth forces us to recognize that the sexual organs are Aphrodite's essential foundation in earthly life. Indeed, the birth of Aphrodite from male genitalia reminds us of the fact that we have all entered this world of flesh and blood through the same gate.

Botticelli's image offers us a chance to see the birth of Venus, not as an all-at-once event, but, rather, as a process. If you look closely at Aphrodite's face, you can see that she is still dreaming, still coming into consciousness and not yet fully awakened. She's only now arriving at the shore where she is about to receive her floral cape. Unlike the branches in the *Primavera* that are full of fruit, the trees here are still in their first flowering.

Aphrodite is naked, with barely a tie in her golden hair, while the maiden who comes forth to receive her is beautifully dressed, with elegant braids in her carefully coifed hair. The couple on the left has provided the energetic impulse to get Aphrodite ashore, but the maiden who receives her provides the accoutrements of civilization which will complete the birth. They will allow Aphrodite to be transformed from a windswept ingénue who's out at sea to a regal figure who's come into her own. If we imagine Aphrodite ashore, elegantly dressed in her new cape, and the trees in the grove grown heavy with fruit, we're not far from the world of the *Primavera*.

***

In passing, it's worth mentioning this painting could not have been created much before the fifteenth century for a simple reason. Before that, no one knew what Venus looked like. Have a look, for example, at the sculpted image of Venus made in the early 1300s for Giotto's Tower next to the Florence cathedral (Figure 14). Venus is shown in heavy robes as a seated figure with two lovers in the palm of her hand. (The mighty Jove, in this same series, is depicted as a fat friar holding a wineglass and crucifix; others are even funnier.) During the Middle Ages, after centuries of suppression of pagan culture in Christian Europe, the images of the pagan gods were virtually lost. It was only after the Renaissance humanists began excavating antique statues and matching them to their textual descriptions in classical literature that the gods and their images were united once again.

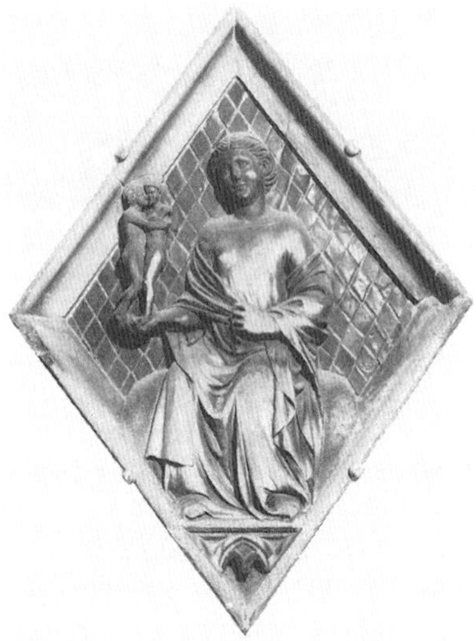

Figure 14: Venus relief on Giotto's Campanile

By the late 15th century, this work of cultural archeology had reached a high level of sophistication, and Botticelli's painting draws on it extensively. Venus was associated with gold and jewelry, with flowers, with pink, with dawn and dusk. Also, much of the classical phenomenology of Venus, as the goddess of love and sexuality, links her with the sea. She was associated with the sea smells of sex, the languorous movements of love and the ebb and flow of desire, the sea-foam, and particularly with the shoreline, where the rhythmic movement of water meets the land, sometimes lapping gently, sometimes plunging forcefully.

Aphrodite was also associated with creatures of the sea like oysters and mollusks and anemones. Based on scent, texture and appearance, and perhaps also for the way they suddenly clam up when stressed, these creatures were considered evocative of the female sex. The next time you visit an aquarium look around for the jellyfish and observe the rhythms of their fluttering veils. As you do so, remember the fluttering of the gowns of the three Graces in Botticelli's *Primavera* and you'll catch a glimpse of the way in which the classical world experienced the presence of Aphrodite.

Botticelli has carefully introduced all these elements into his depiction of the realm of Aphrodite—the clamshell touched with gold, the pink flowers, the shoreline and the sea, the wild eros of young lovers flying through the air, and, of course, the goddess herself in a pose reminiscent of her appearance in classical statuary. But what is utterly amazing about his painting is the way that it affects us: Botticelli's magic invokes the presence of Aphrodite, and we feel it when we stand before his painting. After an absence of a thousand years, the Florentine Renaissance lured Aphrodite back from the archetypal realms to dwell among us for a while...

This is certainly magic enough, but there's still one thing more. Botticelli's image takes one of the dominant metaphors of Western mythology and stands it on its head. We have learned both from Moses and from Aristotle that our spiritual energies are "higher" and our physical desires are "lower". But look carefully at this birth of Venus one more time. The erotic couple on the left, the huffing and puffing lovers, are winged, aerial creatures, and they are blowing *down* their energetic bounty from above. Meanwhile, the flowering, flowered earth maiden on the right stands on her tiptoes and reaches upward to bring her embroidered cape to Aphrodite.

We still have hundreds of years to wait before the poet, William Blake, will dare to say, "The lust of the goat is the bounty of God". Or Patti Smith would sing, "Love is an angel disguised as lust". Yet here in 15th century Christian Florence, we are invited to imagine Heaven descending to bring its gifts of erotic desire. And, perhaps even bolder, we are invited to recognize the intelligent, civilizing energies of the earth rising seamlesslessly from the soil and trees through the flowering maiden to the exquisite artistry of an embroidered cape. Sustained by these forces, and standing upon the waters like a column connecting heaven and earth, Aphrodite brings ashore the gifts of the sacred feminine: love, beauty, compassion and wisdom.

Now that you've been immersed in Botticelli's pagan mythologies, you may be surprised to discover that he is no less skillful, earnest or profound in his exploration of Christian themes.

Botticelli's *Annunciation* imagines the meeting of Mary and Gabriel as a meeting of earth and air, spirit and flesh. The angel seems no less awed at being in Mary's presence than she is of being in his. Look beneath the angel's wings at the way that the gossamer veil over the angel's gown flutters in an imagined breeze while he bends low close to the ground. Then look at Mary. Think of the angel as air, and of Mary as earth. Doesn't the stem of her body look like the calyx of a bulb, newly risen from the earth and slowly opening to the light?

You may remember from the earlier discussion of Simone Martini's *Annunciation* (located in Room 3) that in paintings of this type we typically find some kind of barrier or division that separates Gabriel and Mary. In Botticelli's painting there are several lines of demarcation between the angel and Mary that are crossed on the way to her acceptance. Whereas Simone's painting focused on the first moments of the encounter, Botticelli looks at the moment when Mary is first saying, "Yes." And this silent "Yes," conceived in the soul before being expressed in words, is subtly and beautifully depicted through the various ways in which the boundary lines between Mary and Gabriel are crossed.

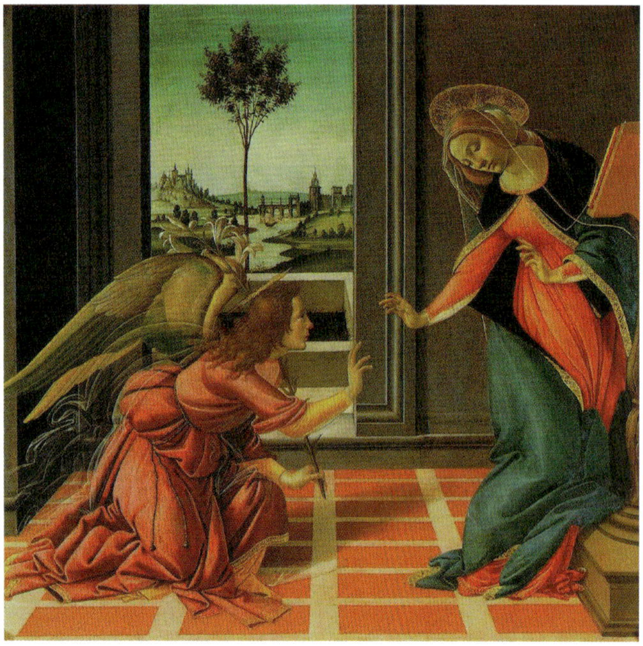

Figure 15: Botticelli's *Annunciation*

Note the vertical line that comes right toward us in the middle of the painting. The tip of the stem of the angel's lily reaches this far, and the rest of his body remains behind this line. Except, of course, for his right hand which reaches across to the edge of the windowed space as his fingertips extend ever so slightly beyond it. This doorway frame divides Mary's interior space from the greater world of rivers and mountains and cities that provides the backdrop for the angelic visitor.

Mary's space is delimited primarily by the rightmost vertical running between the tiles; her pink dress touches it while her blue cloak falls just beyond it. The doorframe has an ornamental element that looks like a reversed "L," and, at her furthest point of extension, Mary's hand just crosses this line, almost meeting Gabriel's. Their palms are already turned toward each other, and the whole drama of the painting focuses on bridging the small distance that remains between their hands.

The reversed "L" design is an ornamental motif that you can still see in the *Ospedale degli Innocenti*, the foundling hospital, that Brunelleschi designed early in the 15th century. In the image before us it serves to draw the eye down from Mary's hand toward the angel's, and it heightens the sense we have of them reaching toward each other despite the obvious hesitancy that each exhibits. And it's the exquisite tension between their modesty and reserve, and that unseen force we sense pulling them toward each other, that gives this image much of its remarkable poignancy.

While this all takes place, the most significant boundary crossing occurs almost unnoticed. It's the angel's shadow which actually extends all the way into Mary's space. Its significance is confirmed by the Latin words painted across the predella of the painting which translate in the King James as: "The Holy Spirit shall come upon thee, and the power of the highest shall overshadow thee."

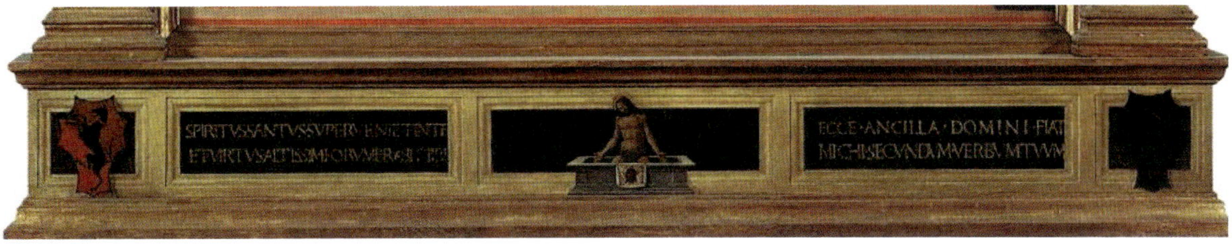

These are the final words that the angel speaks to Mary, and they conclude his visit just as the "Ave Maria" begins it. In scenes that attempt to show her ecstasy in the moment of her acceptance, these same words are sometimes shown in raised gold letters running from the angel toward Mary. They indicate the actual or immanent completion of the angel's mission, much as the words inscribed here beneath the image of Mary indicate her willingness to become the servant of the Lord.

Through the window in this painting, which is open to the elements, you can see earth, air, and water. We are invited to supply the missing fourth by imagining that spark of divine fire that passes between their palms.

The theme of the Adoration of the Magi was an especially important one for the Medici rulers of Florence who made ongoing efforts to associate themselves in the minds of the public with the three kings who came bearing precious gifts. Cosimo the Elder sponsored a procession on Epiphany every year, the twelfth day of Christmas, ostensibly to honor the Christ Child. Epiphany was held to be the day on which the three kings arrived to worship the baby Jesus, and the procession was a reenactment of the event in which people dressed up like the three wise men and their entourage—probably like something right out of Gentile da Fabriano's *Adoration*.

Everyone walked from the Medici Palace to the Medici neighborhood church of San Marco. Cosimo had evicted San Marco's previous tenants on a flimsy pretext and had given the San Marco complex to the Dominicans, who were his staunch supporters. As a token of their gratitude, the Dominicans gave Cosimo personal use of a two-room corner suite in the monastery. Cosimo's room featured a fresco by Fra Angelico and associates which depicted, surprise, the Adoration of the Magi.

Although the Medici were never actually so brazen as to play the parts of the three Magi in the public procession, the association was not lost on anyone. Meanwhile, in the frescoes and altarpieces which they commissioned, they were much less circumspect.

In reading Botticelli's painting of the Adoration, his contemporaries quickly established the *People* magazine tradition (which is still carried on faithfully by modern commentators) of guessing who's who in the picture. The smart money has it that Cosimo the Elder is the one kneeling before the babe, the man with the reddish shirt in the left foreground is probably Lorenzo the Magnificent (though some people think he's the figure in the white cloak who stands directly behind Cosimo while others think he's the dark-haired figure in profile on the right with a red stripe on his black sleeve) and so on and so forth. In this privileged glimpse of the lifestyles of the rich and famous, we get to observe their lavish style of dress and elegant bearing. We may also notice that many of them appear somewhat distracted and are engaged in chit-chat.

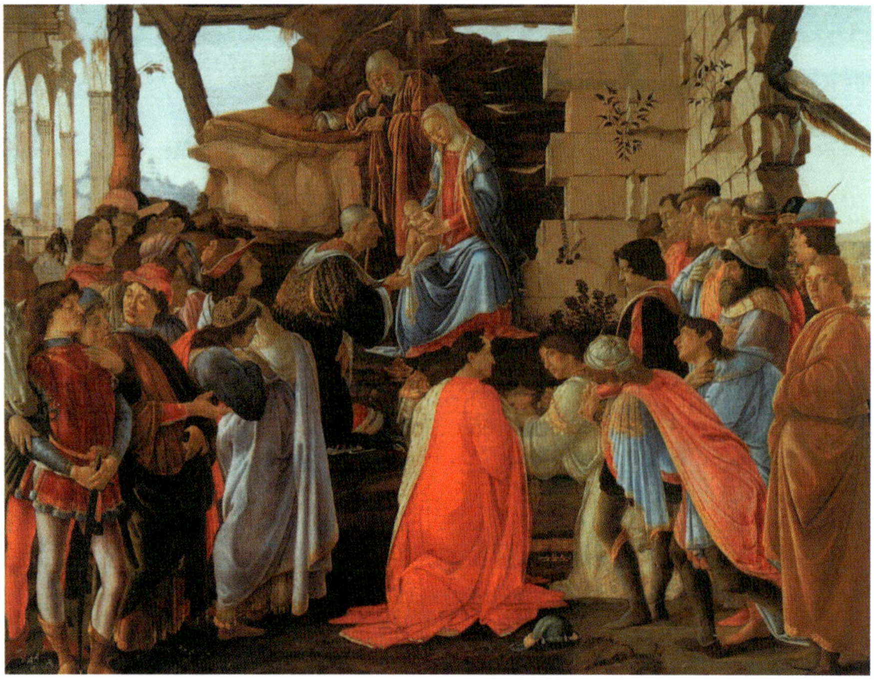

Figure 16: Botticelli's *Adoration of the Magi*

Among the various figures in the crowd there are a couple who look out toward us as if scanning to see whether we've noticed them. Remember Filippo Lippi on the far left of his *Coronation of the Virgin* (back in Room 8) with his head propped up in his hand looking out at us? Well, look at the far right front corner and you'll find Botticelli himself staring out at us in much the same way. Amidst all the multi-colored vestments and gold-embroidered finery, he wears a plain brown cloak and gazes toward us with a sallow, dyspeptic look.

You may be aware that in his later years Botticelli had a difficult time holding together the mystical paganism and reverent Christianity that seemed to blend together so seamlessly during the earlier part of his life. But, in this respect, he simply mirrored the divorce that was happening between these two cultural streams in the larger world. In the time of Cosimo the Elder, the mystical Christianity of San Marco thrived alongside of Cosimo's deep love of classical learning and esoteric philosophy. By the time of Lorenzo the Magnificent, Cosimo's grandson, the alliance was over, and San Marco's Prior, the monk Savanarola, regularly denounced Lorenzo as a tyrant and an irreligious soul. After Lorenzo's death in 1492, Botticelli came fully under Savanarola's influence and was even persuaded to cast some of his paintings into the infamous "Bonfires of the Vanities," which were to meant to purge Florence of its decadence.

In the present painting, done almost 20 years before the bonfires, I think you can already see signs of the coming spiritual schism. Although he is sponsored and sustained by the Medici circle, Botticelli's displeasure with the appropriation of religious themes for profane purposes seems plainly apparent.

I have to confess that I sometimes find Leonardo's work nearly inscrutable, as if he was careful to hide his intent from the prying eyes of the viewer in the same the way he used reversed mirror writing to keep his notes secret. If cryptography is not a form of mystery that you particularly enjoy, your patience for deciphering Leonardo's work may find its limits. Yet, once you get into the spirit of cracking the da Vinci code, the subtlety of the clues he provides toward reading the deeper meaning of his work makes for an interesting adventure. And, in any event, his amazing powers of observation and his extraordinary skill in rendering are worthy of universal admiration.

Leonardo's *Annunciation* may seem somewhat impersonal and unemotional when you first look at it. Rest assured, it still seems that way even after you look at it for years. Unlike other Annunciates who raise their hands in alarm or clutch at their robes, this Mary calmly raises one hand receptively and never loses her place in her book. If there's a lack of dramatic interaction between Mary and Gabriel, it's because Leonardo is not concerned with their personal psychology. He wants to keep us focused on the cosmic and historical dimensions of the drama being enacted, not on the interaction between the actors.

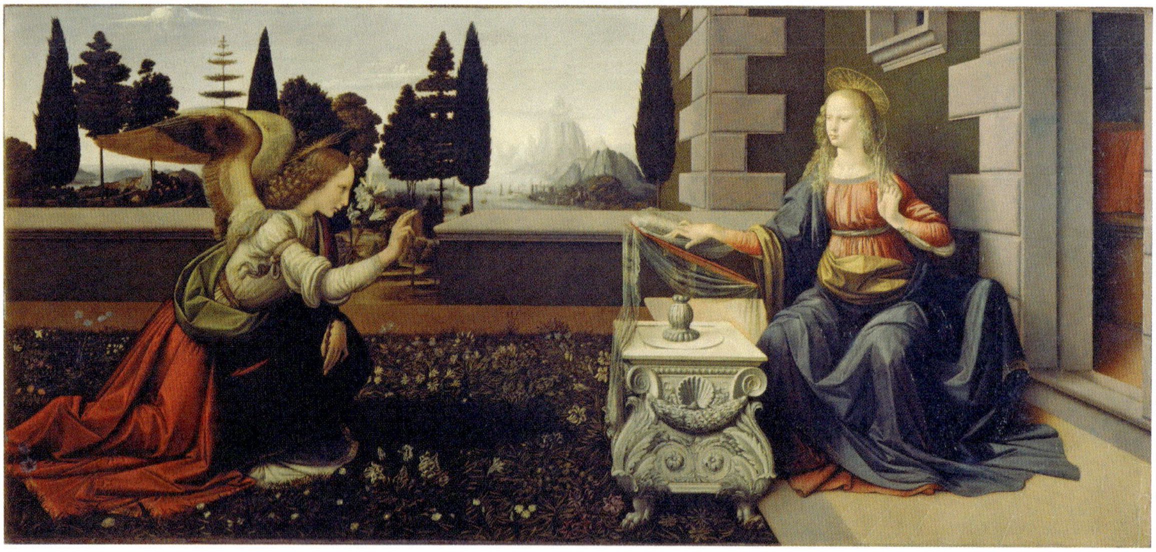

Figure 17: Leonardo da Vinci's *Annunciation*

Leonardo chose to stage his Annunciation at dawn, at the moment of the sun's first rising. If you're fortunate enough to visit the Uffizi on a sunny day when the sun filters through the skylights in the room, it will help you see the play of light in Leonardo's painting. If you find yourself here on a dark grey day, you may just have to take my word for what follows.

Look at the trees and landscape behind the angel, and you'll see that they are bathed in the first rays of the morning light. Try to remember the last time you were up at dawn looking at rocks, trees and shrubs, and you'll see how perfectly Leonardo has captured it. Keep looking at the landscape for a moment and you can almost feel the sun rising.

In the Botticelli *Annunciation* we looked at in the last room, you may recall that the open window onto the outside world was located just behind the kneeling angel. The implications of this motif are that the event initiated by the angel's visit will have repercussions far and wide in the greater world beyond Mary's chamber. In Leonardo's image this theme is once again suggested, this time by the gap in the wall of the Virgin's enclosed garden, just behind the angel.

Based on the angel's shadow, we can infer that the sun is rising directly behind him. In passing, take a moment to admire the lovely way Leonardo has captured the sheen of the angel's red cape in this light. In the garden surrounding the angel the lighting of the flowers is worked out with an almost unbelievable degree of detailed accuracy. Look carefully at the lighting in the garden itself, and you'll notice that there's a subtle but steady increase in the luminosity of the grass and flowers as we move toward Mary. Look at the lawn behind the angel and compare it with the section in front of him, and you'll see the difference.

Now, this is the exact opposite of what should be happening, since the light moves from east to west (here, left to right) as the sun rises. It's also interesting that the lighting changes again when we pass from the natural world of grass and wildflowers to the human world of art and architecture, represented by the elegant *palazzo* and the patio with its carefully laid tile. The golden natural light which floods the garden stops at its edge, and we find a whiter, more diffuse light surrounding Mary. It's as if we are witnessing a reversal, or suspension, of the natural order of things.

***

Because all Annunciations are about the encounter of the human and the Divine, they typically have a dividing line to demarcate these realms, a threshold which clearly separates the angel's space from Mary's. And although this separation is represented in many different ways, the crossing of the threshold always remains the reason for the Angel's visit. Here, located right on the boundary line between the two realms, we find a strange piece of marble furniture with elaborately carved ornamentation.

Let's look more closely at this interesting piece of furniture. Its decorative motifs are drawn from pagan sources. And although its form is square rather than oblong, the design is reminiscent of a Roman sarcophagus. Emerging from this classical base is a slender column which supports the lectern on which Mary reads the Bible. One way of interpreting this image would be to see it as symbolizing the emergence of Christianity from the death of pagan culture. One might compare it, for example, to the ruins of Roman temples that we see in Nativity scenes. But, unlike its kindred motifs in the triumphalist narrative of Christianity, this image adds a subtle twist: it invites us to appreciate the artistry and the elegant geometry of the classical foundation that sustains and supports the Christian revelation.

Finally, take a close look at the Bible which sits on top of the lectern, and look at the way that the Virgin is turning the pages of her book. If you brought your binoculars, you can see that several pages are still settling that have just been flipped from left to right. Indeed, Mary appears to be making her way from the back toward the front of the book where her thumb holds it open.

How are we supposed to understand this? If we remember that Hebrew is written from right to left, and that Hebrew books are read from back to front, it's possible that Leonardo may be simply indicating that Mary, who, of course, was Jewish, would have read the Bible in this manner. Yet since the text is written in Latinate rather than Hebrew letters, it invites us to consider that the Annunciation is the moment when one thing began to turn into another, as the Hebrew Bible of Jerusalem was transmogrified into the Christian Bible of Rome. (And, who knows, there might also be an allusion here to Leonardo's predilection for mirror writing in which everything is read from the opposite direction.)

In any event, we have a reversal that echoes the reversal of natural lighting in the garden. There's the reminder in all this that the Annunciation itself is ultimately an *opus contra naturam*, an event which defies the natural order of things. The angel in the garden with his merely natural bird's wings hails the unnaturally pregnant Virgin at her lectern, and a new order is inaugurated.

Before leaving Room 15, stop and have a look at Perugino's *Agony in the Garden*. Although much of Perugino's work seems somewhat formulaic, his poignant evocation of Christ's ordeal in Gethsemane is very much worthy of admiration. Even with the distraction of the awkward, spindly figures in the background, this is still a compelling painting.

You may recall that on the night before he is arrested, Jesus spends the night in the garden of Gethsemane. His disciples intend to be vigilant and stay awake all night in case they need to defend him, but, actually, they all quickly fall asleep. As he prays, Jesus is visited by an angel who presents him with a cup to drink that symbolizes his destiny. After asking if there's not some way to avoid what lies ahead, he acquiesces and accepts his fate.

The disciples are beautifully rendered in the slackness and torpor of their bodies and the peacefulness of sleep shown on their faces. Only Jesus is awake, alone, outlined against the sky, while his disciples slumber on the ground below. His serenity would seem complete but for the odd twist of his left foot which hints at an inner tension.

The long shadows of early morning light let us know that the moment draws close. The angel comes streaming through the air with downcast glance in the role of fatal messenger, bringing the cup of destiny. The beautiful rendering of Christ's face as he seeks to fathom the mystery and necessity of what awaits him is surely one of the most eloquent passages in Renaissance painting.

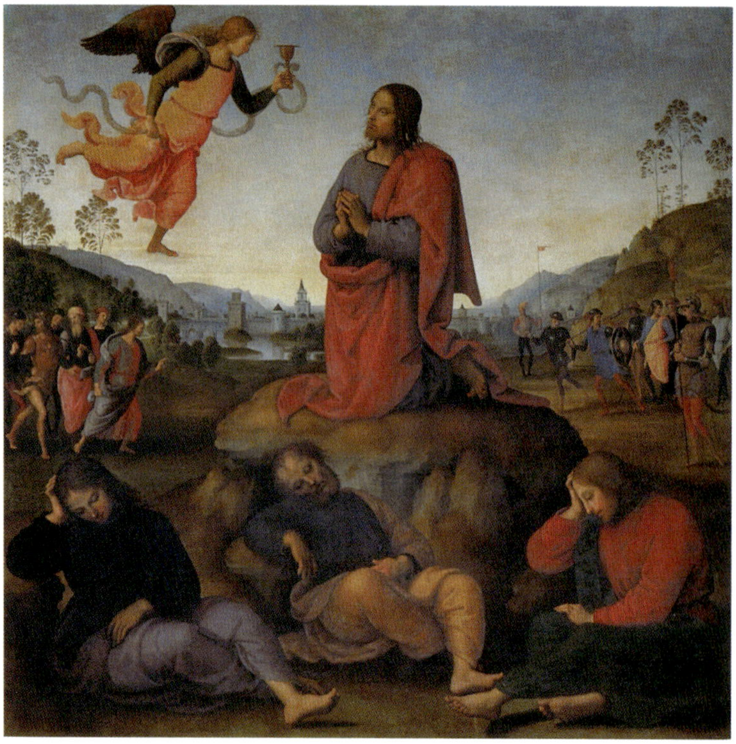

Figure 18: Perugino's *Agony in the Garden*

On the wall directly opposite Perugino's paintings is a curious work by Piero di Cosimo known as the *Incarnation of Christ*. Although Piero's painting seems at first like a typically pious work, the more you look at it, the odder it gets. Apart from its own merits, Piero's work is intriguing because you can see the faultlines of some of the major changes that will arrive in the decades ahead.

Prior to this work, the Incarnation was always implied in paintings of the Annunciation. But, here, it is broken out on its own: the Dove floods Mary with its light as she puts her hand over her womb. The Annunciation is acknowledged in relief on the pedestal on which Mary stands, but it's treated almost as if it is a separate event.

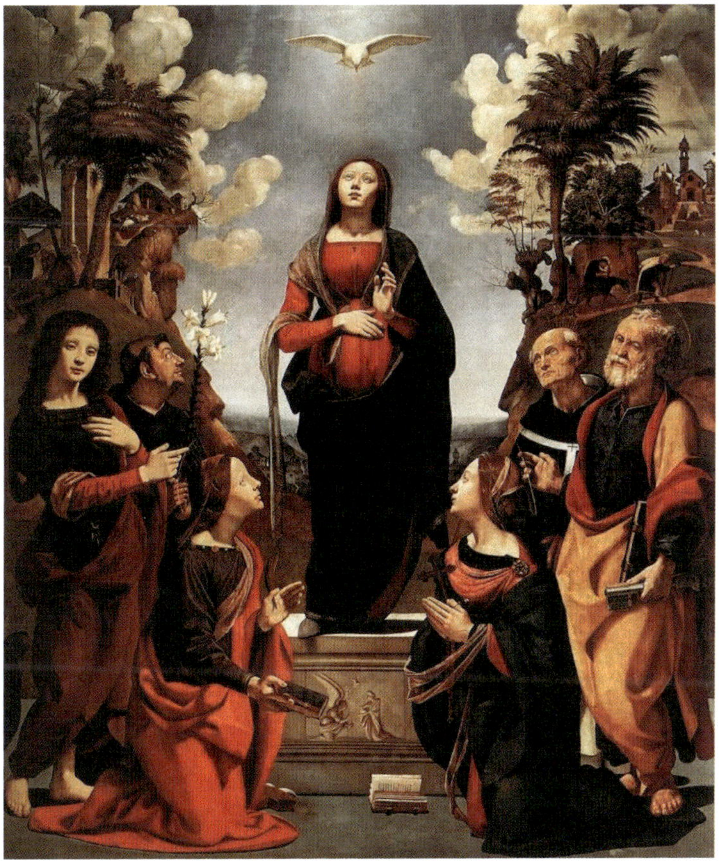

Figure 19: Piero di Cosimo's *Incarnation of Christ*

Also unusual are the background scenes with their strange trees and tiny houses perched on the edge of impossible cliffs. The exaggerated symmetry of the hills, trees and clouds helps to create a sense of unreality, as do the tiny scenes on the hills where we see future events such as the Nativity and the Flight into Egypt.

Piero's *Incarnation* is painted around the turn of the 16th century, and he draws skillfully on the broad range of representational techniques developed in Florence over the past century to show us the "real" world. But, perhaps deliberately, he does so in a way that subverts their usual intention. So we find ourselves neither in heaven nor on earth. Instead, we seem to be in a world where the artist is enjoying his ability to create a fictive universe and to bend and flaunt the rules of plausibility and verisimilitude as he chooses. We'll see much more of this in coming decades when we look at paintings by the Mannerists.

For the moment, it's worth noting that we've come full circle in some strange way. Medieval icons like Duccio's *Madonna* were clearly designed as ritual objects and were not intended to represent the world around us. Then, the Florentine Renaissance brought the scenes of sacred drama down from heaven and situated them in a world that looks like our own. In the final phase of the Renaissance, which Piero's painting hints at, painting once again divorces itself from the real world. But, instead of returning to heaven, it now seems to realize that it constitutes a world of its own and can make its own rules. Welcome to the World of Art.

Before we move on, notice the difference in feeling when Mary is put on a pedestal. She becomes almost like a statue of herself. No longer the honored member of a congregation, or the queen of the heavenly court, she becomes an object of worship. After spending some time on earth during the 15th century, we see her at the end of the century moving back up toward heaven, set apart once more from mere mortals like us.

After exiting the Leonardo Room, continue your walk down the First Corridor until you come to the entrance to the Tribuna. It's a hexagonal room with walls covered in red fabric, and it's filled with statues and paintings. Take a moment to stop and look up at the ceiling in this amazing room. You may not believe it, but those are seashells that you're looking at. The room is decorated to conform to the schema of the four elements: the lantern windows at the very top represent "air"; the seashells and their accompanying motifs suggest "water"; the red walls are, of course, "fire", and the inlaid stones of the pavement are symbols of the earth.

If you look across the room, you can see a famous statue of Aphrodite known as the Medici Venus. She stands in the classic pose known as the *Venus Pudica* or "modest Venus" upon which, as many have noted, Botticelli based his figure in *The Birth of Venus*. But Botticelli made one important change that radically shifts the reading of his image. Rather than concealing her breasts "unsuccessfully"—which is the erotic subtext of the classical pose—Botticelli's Venus is actually placing her hand over her heart.

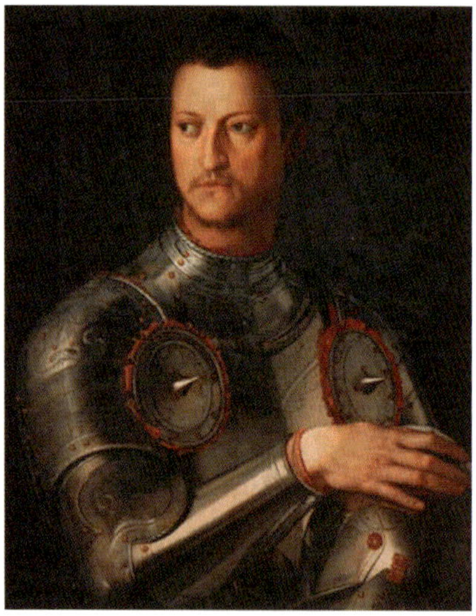

Figure 20: Bronzino's *Portrait of Duke Cosimo I*

Up on the walls is a portrait of Duke Cosimo I by Bronzino. Bronzino depicts him as a man of intelligence and culture with more interest in power than love. The spiked breasts pointedly suggest that he was not the nurturing type, and his well-known ruthlessness toward his foes confirms the visual hint that he's not someone you'd want to get too close to.

On your way out of the Tribuna, look up to the left of the doorway and you'll see Rosso Fiorentino's little guitar-playing angel, the one that has found its way onto a million greeting cards. I sometimes imagine Rosso turning in his grave, lamenting that he lived before the age of commercial syndication.

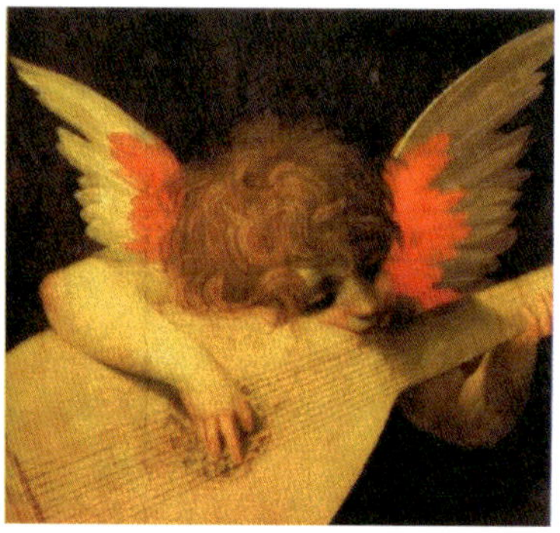

Figure 21: Rosso Fiorentino's *Guitar-Playing Angel*

As you exit from the Tribuna, you'll be entering Room 19. On the wall across from you, on your left, is a delightful painting by Piero di Cosimo. It depicts the story of the courageous hero, Perseus, the helpless heroine, Andromeda, and the villainous sea monster who threatens to devour her. The monster has a wonderful corkscrew tail and snorts and salivates in frustrated anticipation while he awaits the final blow that will dispatch him.

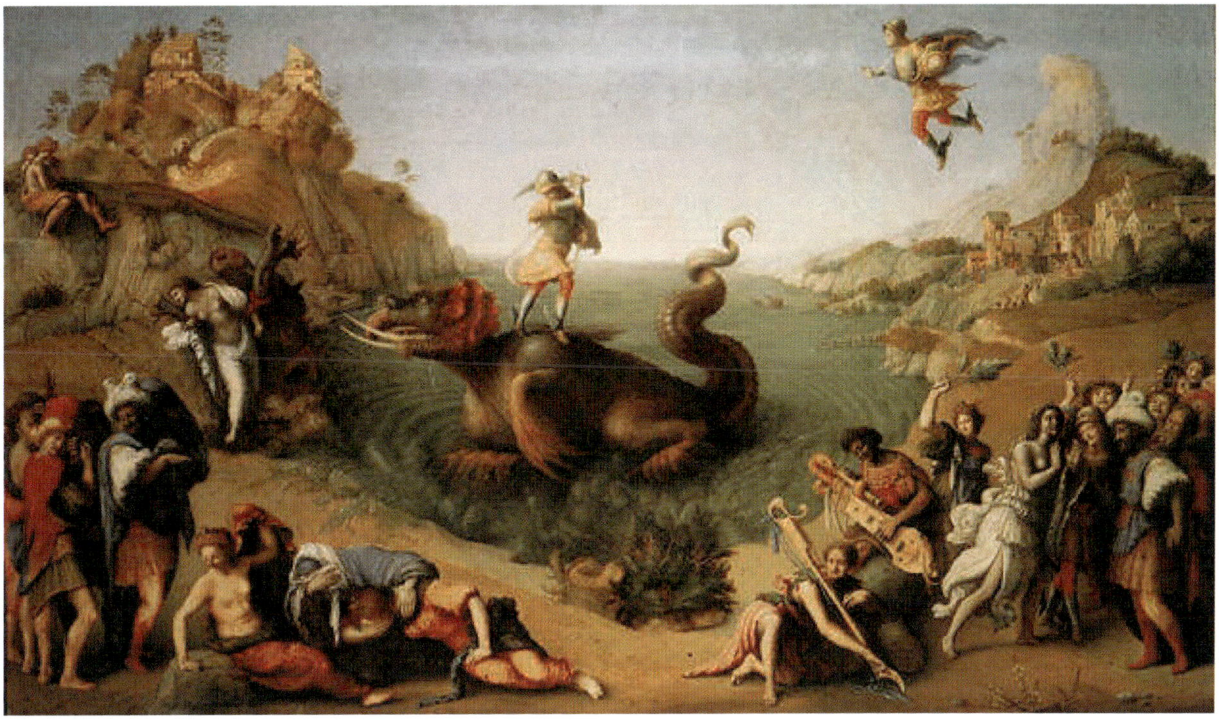

Figure 22: Piero di Cosimo's *Liberation of Andromeda*

On the shore, Piero has staged a melodrama. On the right side, the crowd cheers wildly as Perseus flies in overhead. On the left side, the crowd cowers and shields its eyes as the climactic moment approaches: will the Virgin be gored by the tusks of the lascivious monster or will the hero rescue her in time?

We can see that Piero definitely amused and entertained himself with his paintings. The people on the right are playing entirely fictitious instruments that could never make a sound. And, as in many of his paintings, improbable houses stand high on impossible cliffs. "So what?," the artist seems to suggest. "Those houses don't have to withstand winter's storms. And the instruments can play any kind of music you like. Don't you realize it's a painting?"

In Piero's work we hear the early notes of the refrain that would become, for better and certainly for worse, the rallying cry of modern artists: Art can be whatever we want it to be!

Albrecht Durer and Lukas Cranach: *Adam and Eve* — Room 20

Room 20 features the work of some of the great Northern European masters of the 16th century. There are two beautiful sets of panels depicting the Temptation of Adam and Eve. One set is by Lukas Cranach, and the other set is a workshop copy of originals painted by Albrecht Durer.

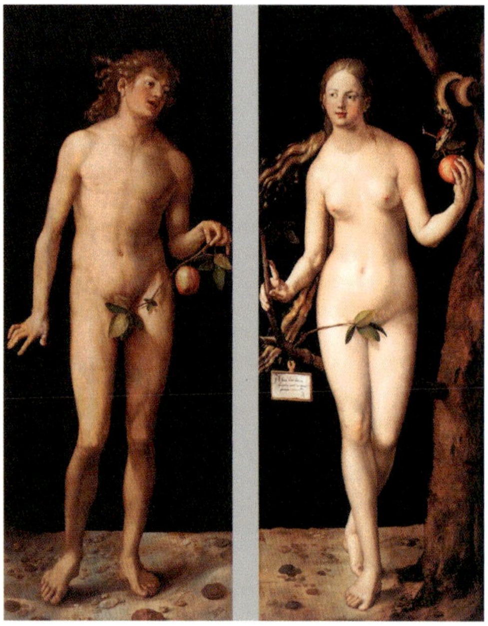

Figure 23: Workshop of Albrecht Durer: *Adam and Eve*

Note that Adam and Eve are eating apples as they always do in Northern Europe. In Italy they always eat figs. It's interesting that in Italian the names of most fruits are feminine, (*mela, pera, albicocca*—apple, pear, apricot) while the names of the trees that bear the fruit are masculine (*melo, pero, albicocco*). A notable exception is made for the fig, where tree and fruit are both masculine (*fico, fico*). If you ever want to embarrass your Italian friends, ask them why they don't use the feminine form for the fruit and watch them squirm.

In Durer's painting, it's not clear that they've eaten the apples yet. But there seems to be the suggestion that simply taking them in hand was enough to open their eyes. There's the sense in all this of a thrilling moment: Eve's hair curls wildly, and Adam looks joyously alive. This seems to be the moment when the realm of truly human being separates itself from the dim world of nature. How great the distance has grown between Eve and the beast who slumbers at her feet, between Adam and the stag who looks out at us with the dark, mute eye of nature.

In Cranach's version, which was done later than Durer's originals, we get to see Eve immediately after the Fall. It's fun to look at her face and imagine what she is feeling and what she is thinking as she offers the apple to Adam. If you look closely at the apple she holds in her hand, you can see the little teethmarks where she's just taken her first bite.

Eve tempts while Adam ponders.
The rest is history.

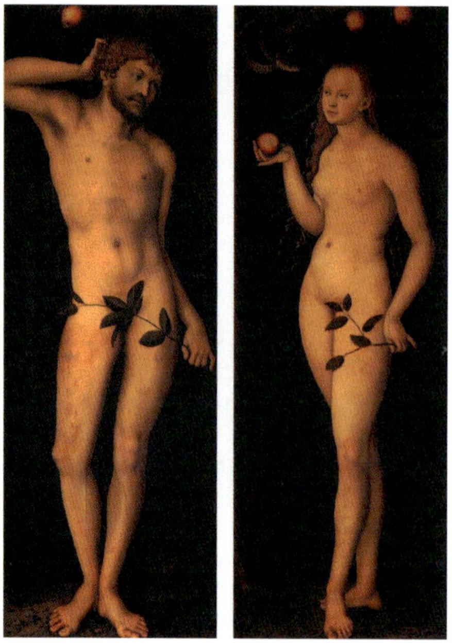

Figure 24: Lukas Cranach: *Adam and Eve*

Mark Helprin fans may remember a Giorgione painting known as *The Tempest* which figured so prominently in Helprin's novel, *A Hero of the Great War.* Though it seems that no one agrees on the meaning of the painting or whom the figures are supposed to represent, this has not kept the painting from capturing the fancy of generations of admirers.

Giorgione is one of those artists who was so widely admired during his time—and who had so many imitators and disciples—that the challenge of identifying those works actually done by Giorgione's own hand has been formidable. Over the years the number of certifiable Giorgiones has sharply diminished as new questions are raised about the authenticity of certain works. Fortunately, those of us who are neither gallery owners nor insurance specialists don't need to be overly preoccupied with these issues, and we can feel at liberty to enjoy both Giorgione and the "Giorgionesque."

I had the good fortune some years ago of attending a talk on Giorgione given by Norman Coady, a Lecturer at the National Gallery in London. Two works were discussed: the first, an Adoration of the Magi, was certainly by Giorgione, whereas the second work was of somewhat doubtful attribution. Apropos its authenticity, Mr. Coady reminisced that whenever the late Sir Kenneth Clark would pass by the painting, he would always say "It must be a Giorgione"! Which is to say that it certainly wasn't. But, as it was such an inspired imitation, we might as well enjoy it!

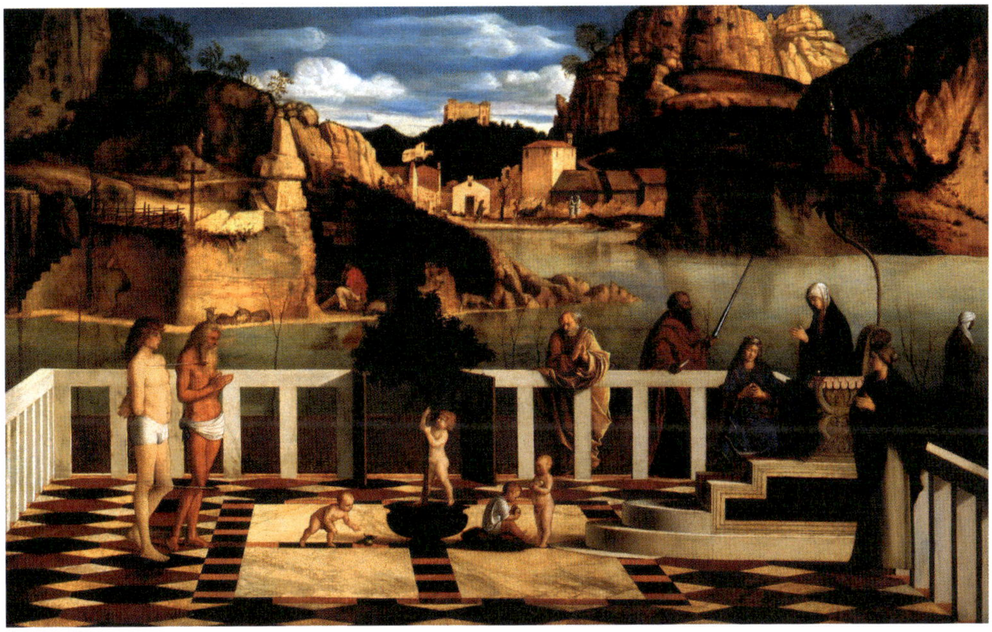

Figure 25: Bellini's *Sacred Allegory*

In much of Giorgione's work, as well as in certain of Bellini's paintings like the *Sacred Allegory* shown here, there is a subtly crafted air of enchantment. Their feeling of mystery accounts for much of these works' appeal and is precisely what induced so many other artists to try to emulate their magic spell. Meanwhile, enormous effort has been spent on trying to explicate various symbols and themes, which seems to me to be largely beside the point. The play's the thing: enjoy the show.

When you're ready to move on, walk right through the next room, don't stop to look at *The Martyrdom of St. Florian*, and continue on into Room 23 where you'll see *Leda and the Swan* on the far wall on your left.

Leda and the Swan is the copy of a painting by Leonardo da Vinci, the original of which has disappeared without a trace. Not only is the composition apparently faithful to the original, but the style is also very "Leonardesque," so it's the next best thing to having the original in front of you.

Behold the proud parents as they stand over their hatchlings. From the union of the immortal Jove, who has taken the form of a swan, and the mortal maiden, Leda, two sets of twins are born. In the background are the two boys, Castor and Pollux; in the foreground are the two girls, Helen and Clytemnestra. Helen may still be a bit young for you to realize that this was the face that launched a thousand ships. Yes, this is the very same Helen that Paris would run off with years later to precipitate the tragic events of the Trojan War.

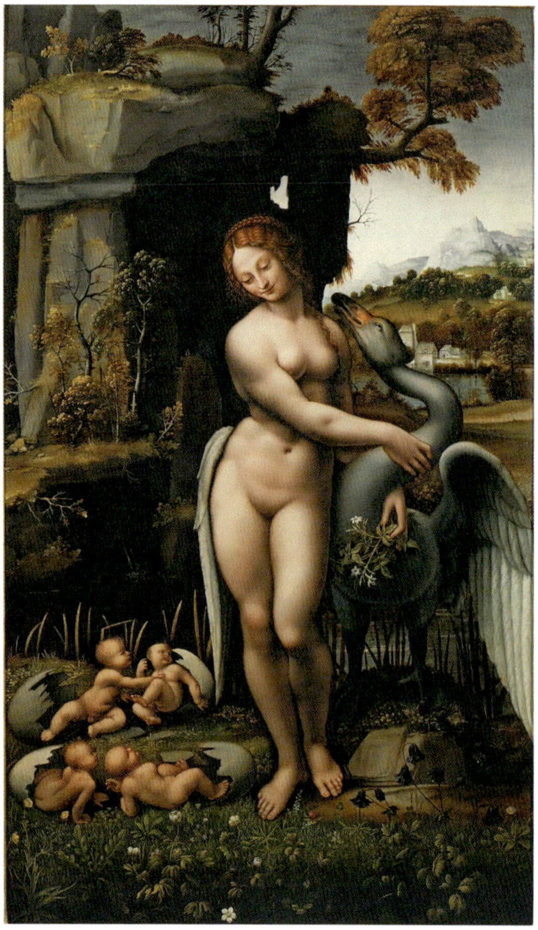

Figure 26: Leonardo da Vinci (copy):
Leda and the Swan

Notice how the two boys look up directly at their immortal father, while the twin girls look to their mortal mother. Meanwhile, Jove's wing embraces Leda affectionately, and his beak nuzzles almost comically toward her with an aching tenderness. Or, is his upward glance a hint that, having feathered the nest and fathered the brood, it's high time to return to Olympian heights? A curious creature, this god-swan, both more and less than human.

The great poet, William Butler Yeats, understood the union of Leda and the Swan to be the generative act that inaugurated the age of the Mycenaean Greeks. It was the foundation myth of that pagan universe in the same way that the Annunciation to Mary served as the foundation of the Christian story. And it's interesting that in both stories the divine assumes the form of a bird in consummating the union with the mortal maiden.

What was it that inspired Leonardo to depict such a strange topic? Think for a moment of Joseph, Mary and the infant Jesus. Try to keep The Holy Family in mind as you look at this picture, and I think you will see that Leonardo could not resist the challenge of imagining the pagan counterpart to the Christian Nativity scene!

As is the case with many of Leonardo's paintings, Michelangelo's depiction of the Holy Family, known as the *Doni Tondo* ("tondo" meaning "round") can be exasperating in its subtlety. After centuries of speculation, we're certain only that all is not as it seems and that there's more here than meets the eye.

Let's start with some of the more accessible aspects. Notice how the Holy Family is set off from the group of figures who linger in the background by a low grey border of stone on which Joseph appears to be sitting. This grey stone looks like the upper edge of some sort of retaining wall which separates the grassy area above from the sunny balcony below where the young John the Baptist stands looking upwards.

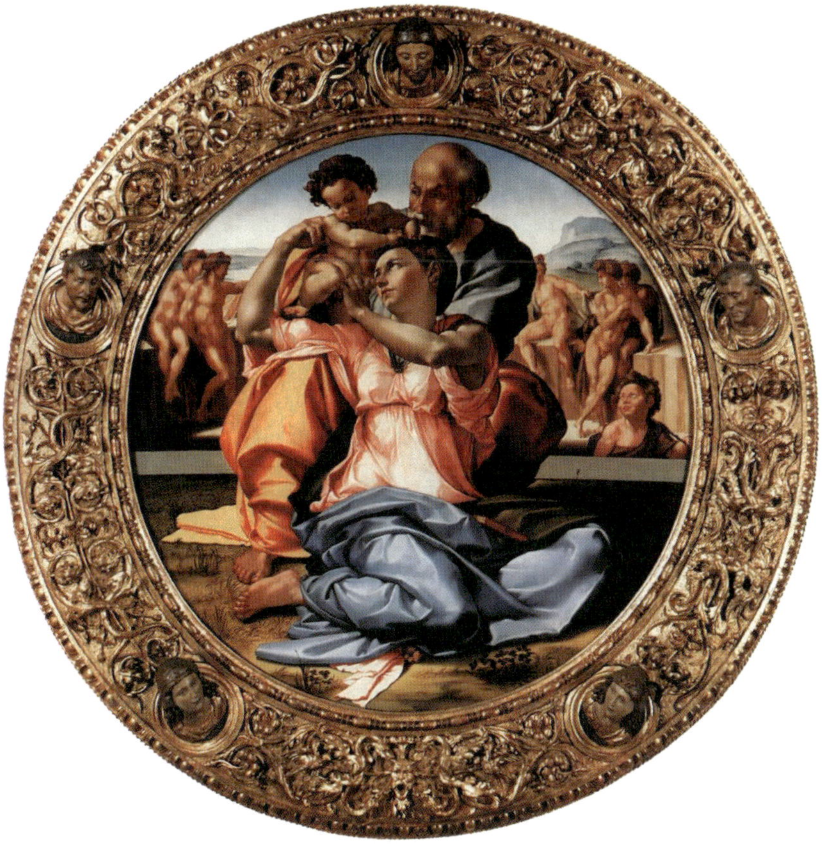

Figure 27: Michelangelo's *Doni Tondo*

So, who are these naked guys in the background and what are they doing here? They exhibit a casual non-chalance about their nudity, and the couple on the right appears to be snuggled in a sort of homoerotic embrace. It's the kind of thing you might expect at one of Socrates' banquets. And, just to be sure that we understand he is referring to the pre-Christian pagan world, Michelangelo even bases some of the postures of his nudes on classical sculptures that were being retrieved in his day.

Like Leonardo's lectern in his *Annunciation* with its classical base supporting the Bible above it, Michelangelo shows us the classical back-ground to the Christian story which has superseded it. Yet, it's interesting that we find the baby Jesus here as naked as a pagan, and we see the Madonna barefoot and with her sleeve rolled up on her muscular arm. It's as if Michelangelo celebrates the Incarnation in this image by showing us the grace and beauty of the flesh, and by presenting the Holy Family on the grass, feeling no less at home on the earth and in the body than our pagan forbears.

***

In the images of Madonna and Bambino that you see all through the Uffizi, you may have noticed a certain melancholy undercurrent that runs through many of them. It comes from the fact that both mother and child were understood to be aware of all that lay ahead. Yet, they almost seem to take turns being concerned with it. Sometimes the Christ Child seems to solemnly contemplate his fate while his mother simply fusses with adjusting his blanket. At other times, the babe cavorts innocently on her lap while she gazes fearfully into the future. In otherwise innocent scenes, we often find things like pomegranates or coral that hint darkly at the blood to be shed.

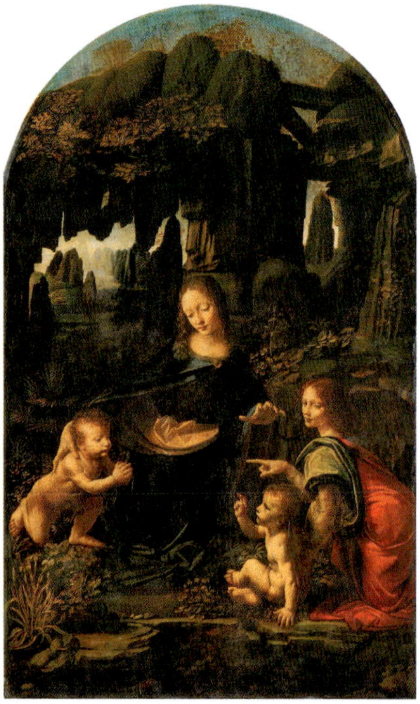

Figure 28: Leonardo's *Madonna of the Rocks*

This theme of foreshadowing is introduced in the present image indirectly and with utmost subtlety. Before exploring its uses in the present context, we'll need to look briefly at a couple of other paintings whose masterful use of indirection established precedents that Michelangelo may have had in mind when he composed the *Doni Tondo.*

Have a look at the picture of Leonardo's *Madonna of the Rocks* which is presently located in the Louvre (Figure 28). Can you make out the invisible Cross formed by the gestures of the four figures? Imagine a line drawn from the angel on the right, through the angel's pointing finger, and to the Christ Child who kneels with his hands outstretched in prayer. Imagine another line that crosses the first running from Mary's palm, through the angel's hand down to the face of the young John the Baptist who is raising his arm and pointing upward. (Meanwhile, Mary's palm, drawn strangely, plays a secondary role as the Hand of Fate, *le griffe effroyable de Dieu,* as the poet Baudelaire once called it.) You may be aware that this same gesture, where John the Baptist points upwards, occurs in other paintings by Leonardo. It was understood that John the Baptist had the gift of foreknowledge of Christ's coming and of his destiny, and in the *Madonna of the Rocks* this awareness is indicated by the invisible Cross that hangs suspended between them all.

This same theme appears in an even more astonishing way in an extraordinary painting by Andrea del Sarto which also hangs in the Louvre. Del Sarto's painting shows us the Madonna and Child with Saints Elizabeth and John the Baptist and two angels (Figure 29).

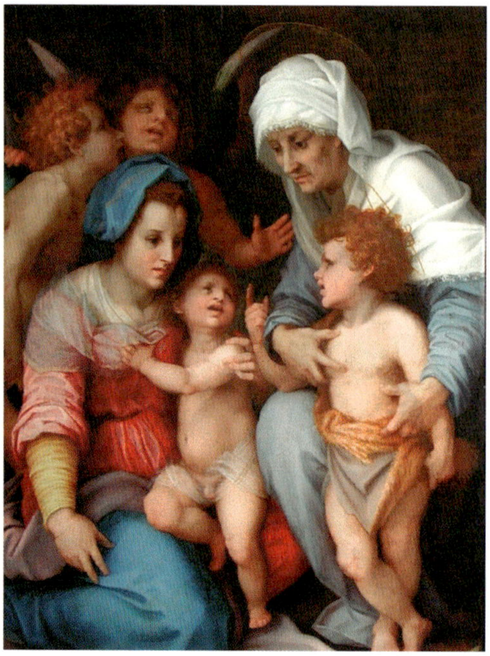

Figure 29: Del Sarto's *Madonna and Child with Saints Elizabeth and John the Baptist and Two Angels*

Look at how Jesus' expression is carefully mirrored in the face of one angel while the other angel has the same reddish curls as the young Baptist. It appears that del Sarto took pains to match each angel to one of the children, as if to suggest that this was not just a visit of angels, but the visit of *their angels*. The visit of the angels coincides with some sort of revelation, as the young John the Baptist points upward and everyone seems to go into an altered state. The Christ Child appears profoundly distraught and Mary and Elizabeth stare vacantly into space as if in trance. We are not shown what they see on the plane of vision, but we are invited to imagine it.

And, now, let's go back for a second look at Michelangelo's work. Not to be outdone in subtlety, Michelangelo invokes the same theme of dark presentiment, but with incomparable understatement. He simply has the infant John the Baptist *look* upward instead of pointing upward.

We're alerted to the significance of lines of sight by the matching figures of angels and prophets with fixed stares whose heads emerge from the frame that Michelangelo designed. If you brought your binoculars, look closely at Mary's face and then at Jesus' face and see where they are looking. You'll notice that the Christ Child seems to be glancing at his own hands. This draws our attention to the fact that he is not reaching out toward his mother, as one might expect, but, instead, is placing his hands on her head as if in an act of transmission. Once again, we cannot know what she sees in this moment, but we can imagine. And we can assume that it's the same vision that has captured the attention of John the Baptist, who obviously can't be staring with such interest at Joseph's back. His inclined head, upturned face and upward glance is perfectly mirrored by the Madonna. Whatever it is that they witness, we can see that it causes Mary's mouth to fall open and her hands to go slack. If a moment earlier she was reaching for her child, her limp, dangling fingers hardly seem capable of holding him now.

***

Much like Leonardo, Michelangelo wants us to see the Christ story in its cosmic dimensions, more than in terms of its personal drama. The form of the painting itself, known as a *tondo*, seems to be chosen as a vehicle for these larger themes. There's a movement in the painting that proceeds from the background toward the foreground. On one level we see it in the passing of the child from Joseph in back to Mary in front; in this sense, Jesus is moving toward our space. On another level it's present in the sequence that leads from the natural world to the pagan world to the Holy Family and then to us who contemplate them. By extending this implicit line perpendicular to the picture plane, the circle aspires toward becoming a sphere. Even in the way the Holy Family is drawn, there's a hint of seeing them as if through a convex, spherical surface.

Now, have a look at the wall on which the nude, young men sit in the background. Notice that it's a semicircular structure. Imagine what would happen if you extended its curvature: it would intersect the picture plane and also add a third dimension to our image. Finally, if you look closely at that wall behind the Holy Family—which appears at first glance to be a straight line—you'll find that it is, in fact, very slightly curved. If you extend it in your imagination, you'll see that it creates an enormous circle. Symbolically speaking, that circle would be only slightly smaller than the world itself. And it would contain, in addition to this first family of Christendom, all those who have stood, over these past two millennia, in the space they first defined.

Mariotto Albertinelli's *Visitation*

Room 25

The episode of the Visitation is based on the Biblical story that immediately follows the Annunciation. The young Mary, realizing that she is now pregnant, makes for the hill country in haste. She seeks out her cousin, Elizabeth, who, although advanced in years, is herself also pregnant (with John the Baptist). As Mary confides her news, the older woman listens empathically and offers her comfort and emotional support.

In Albertinelli's *Visitation*, the columns that frame the meeting are appropriately decorated with birds and babes to remind us of the background to the story. And the smaller scenes in the predella below—the Annunciation, Nativity and Circumcision—also remind us of key milestones in the drama of maternity.

Yet for Albertinelli, as for many other Renaissance artists, the meeting of Mary and Elizabeth offered, above all else, an opportunity to celebrate friendship among women. As we look at Albertinelli's sensitive depiction of their meeting, we can imagine Mary whispering, "You won't believe what just happened to me!" And we see Elizabeth, taking her hand, reassuring her, letting her know that she's there for her, and that she's ready to hear the whole story. A friend in need.

Styles of clothing constantly change, new fashions in architecture may come and go, yet how constant is the human heart...

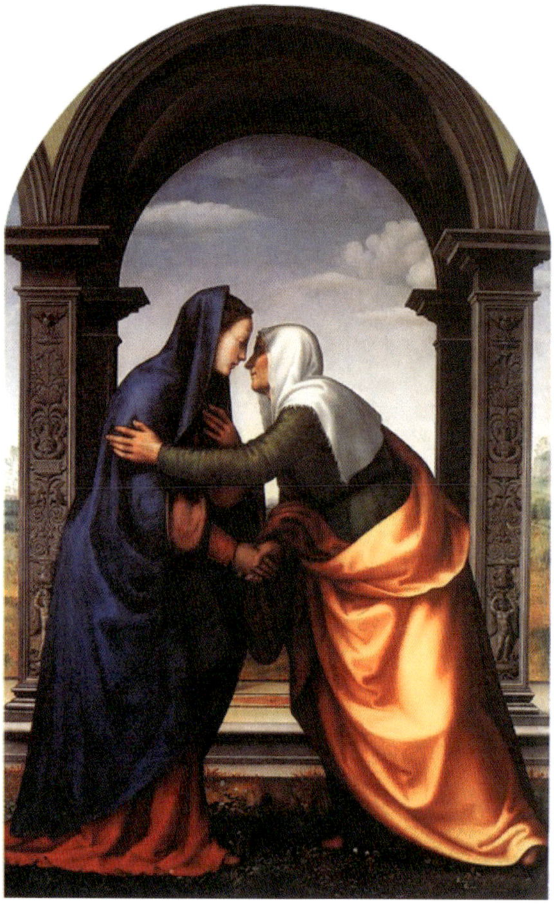

Figure 30: Albertinelli's *Visitation*

Andrea del Sarto's *Madonna of the Harpies* is one of those images that initially looks like a typical, pious contract painting of Mary on a pedestal surrounded by Saints. But, as you look at it, you start to notice odd elements that begin to make you wonder. And, as when trying to understand a dream, it's often the elements that are strange and out-of-place which hold the key to understanding the image.

In Andrea's painting what catches our attention immediately are the strange winged creatures that decorate the pedestal. These were initially described as "harpies" by Giorgio Vasari, the 16th century chronicler of the lives of the great Florentine artists. Through Vasari's writings much of the fact and fiction about their works was passed on to posterity.

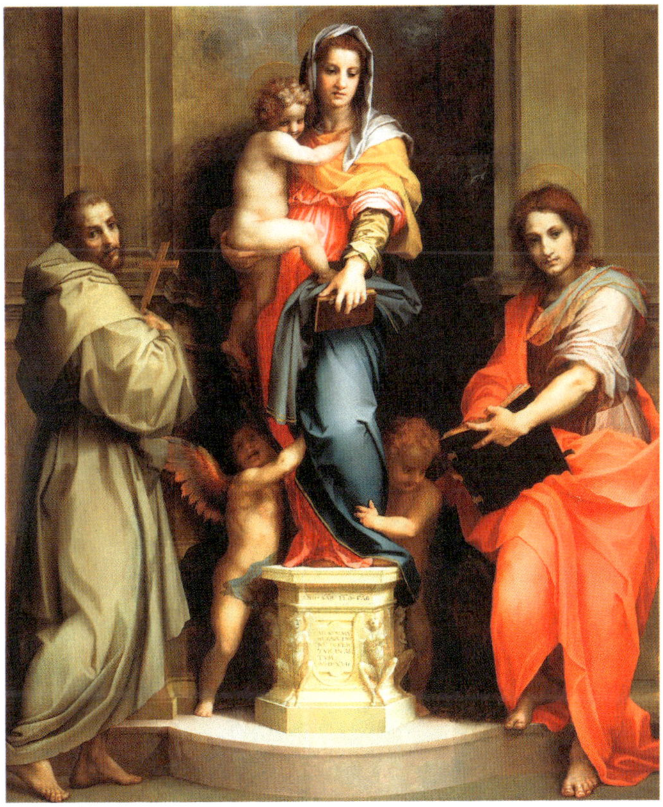

Figure 31: Del Sarto's *Madonna of the Harpies*

You may remember that harpies were conceived in the pagan imagination as hybrid creatures that were half bird and half woman. They were sometimes depicted in a squatting form, like birds on a branch, where the upper body appeared feminine and lovely while the lower was shown with chicken-like legs and sharp talons clinging to the branch.

Contemporary critics, noticing that the lower half of Andrea's creatures is not bird-like, have challenged the traditional identification of these figures as "harpies." Some have argued that they are really sphinxes. Others have suggested that they are locusts and refer to the cloud of locusts mentioned in the Book of Revelations. (You may be wondering, if they are locusts, why they are depicted with women's faces and breasts, why they have cloven hoofs, and why their legs are parted in a way that hardly makes one think about crickets...)

Rather than arguing about whether they are harpies, sphinxes or locusts, let's take another approach. Try this experiment: Hold your hand (or a book) in front of you so that for just a moment you block out the lower half of these creatures' bodies. When you see only their upper torsos, they could almost be mistaken for angels raising their voices in song. Next, shift your hand so that you see only their lower torsos, and you're suddenly in the realm of cloven hoofs and spread legs. Now, keeping in mind the tension between angel and satyr that these creatures embody, let's take a look at other elements of this image that also show the soul pulled in opposite directions.

***

The pedestal that Mary stands on, with its classical mythological motifs and its carved lettering reminiscent of inscriptions on Roman monuments, invokes the familiar theme of Christianity surmounting the pagan world. But the inscription itself, which refers to raising the throne of the Queen on high, alerts us to another level of meaning. According to tradition, the two Cherubim who stand on either side of God's throne always look in different directions. One turns toward God and is occupied with heavenly thoughts while the other gazes earthward and considers the realms below. Take a look now at our two

Cherubs. The one on our left grabs high up on Mary's leg and gazes upward with an imploring look that cries out: "Take me away"! The Cherub on the right holds on to Mary, low on her leg, and gazes downward with interest and absorption.

On our left, St. Francis seems to manifest this same tension, but expressed in a single figure. The Saint, who spoke with the animals and passionately loved the wild places of the earth, faces the throne of heaven, holds the Cross before him, but turns to gaze longingly, almost wistfully, at the world left behind.

There's also an interesting division among the six figures in the painting. Three are youthful, naked, exuberant, and spontaneous in their movements; three are clothed, mature, poised and resigned, carrying with them the artifacts associated with their callings. We see the division between flesh and spirit, between the lure of immanence and the call to transcendence, that echoes the tension embodied by the six figures who decorate the pedestal.

***

Both the Cherubs at the base of the throne as well as the figure of St. Francis were deliberately introduced by del Sarto even though his original contract specified otherwise. The initial contract actually requested that del Sarto depict a later Franciscan Saint who wrote rules for the Order, along with two angels placing a crown on the head of the Madonna. What a different painting that would have been!

Consider finally that this painting was commissioned for a convent chapel, and you can appreciate the relevance of the tensions it explores to the audience it was intended to serve. Instead of the sweet, uplifting image requested by "management", Andrea chose to provide a contemplative image that reflected the existential struggles of the convent dwellers.

The painting appears to be set in the interior of a church with drab walls and a recessed niche in which Mary stands as if aspiring to become like a statue of herself. If you look closely, you can see the wisps of smoke hovering in the air like clouds of incense from the swinging censers that would have accompanied the nun's devotions while they adored the Queen of Heaven on her pedestal. As they did so, we may wonder if some of them were comforted when they noticed that the poignant tensions constellated in this painting were not so very different from their own.

Although he is typically grouped with Leonardo and Michelangelo as the third great master of the High Renaissance, Raphael's work has little in common with the halting, agonized, cerebral complexity of the other two masters but, rather, seems to flow almost effortlessly from his prolific brush.

Among his many masterpieces is this portrait of Giovanni de' Medici, great-grandson of Cosimo the Elder, painted just a few years after Giovanni became Pope Leo X in 1513. Giovanni's election as Pope represented the fulfillment of the highest spiritual aspirations and ambitions of this family which had made its way from farming to commerce to banking and, then, to political power.

Raphael depicts the Pope seated in a handsome upholstered chair flanked by two Cardinals. They stand stiffly on either side of him, almost like sacred statues. The composition recalls depictions of the enthroned Madonna with Saints and thus invokes a sort of "glory by association" for both the Pope and his cohorts. All of this is admirably done, but it is ultimately secondary to Raphael's major concern. His overriding interest is to explore lighting and texture, and his skill at doing so is almost uncanny.

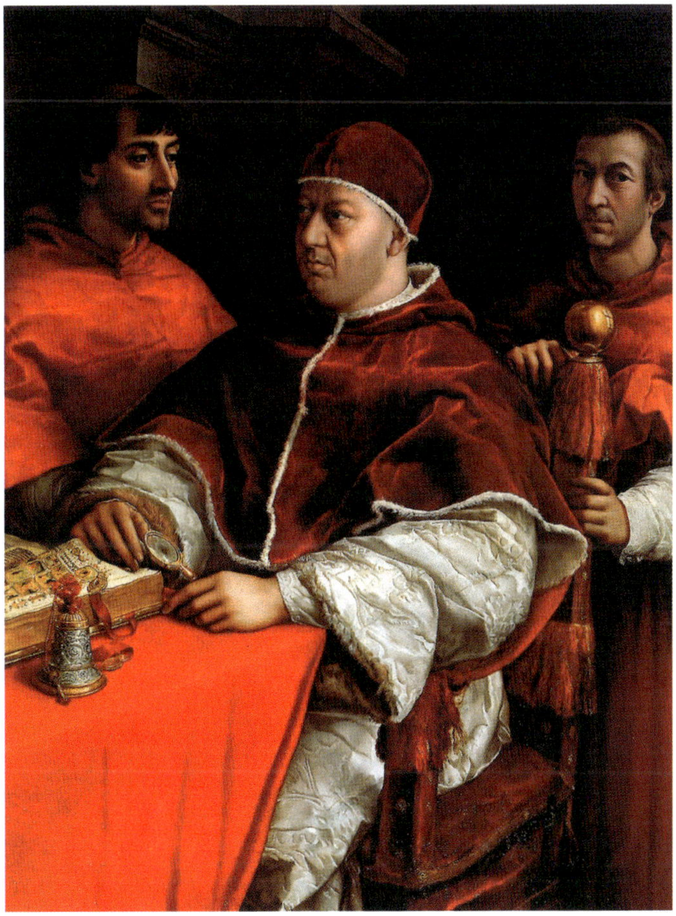

Figure 32: Raphael's *Portrait of Pope Leo X*

Look carefully at the Pope's white damask robe and you'll see that you can tell exactly how stiff the material is, how it would feel to touch it. Now imagine touching his red cap and his cape and notice how much softer this fabric is. Spend a few moments exploring the various surfaces and objects in the painting, mentally touching and handling them. You'll find that Raphael gives us all the information we need in order to know exactly what they will *feel* like, from the bell that invites you to pick it up and ring it, to the lustrous knob on the back of the Pope's chair, to the pale flesh of his sensitive, gentle hands.

This astonishing feat is due in no small measure to Raphael's meticulous observation of the ways in which light reflects on various objects. In this respect he anticipates and is no less extraordinary than the Dutch Masters of the next century who would devote all their energies to exploring the play of light on lemon peels and lobster shells.

Look at the subtlety with which Raphael modulates light and shadow across the various fabric surfaces. Notice that the gilt-edged pages and cover of the Pope's book have a certain luster quite different from the metallic surfaces of the bell which stands beside them. And that these are distinct from the dull sheen of the polished globe on the back of the Pope's chair in which you can see the whole world in reflection like a composition in the key of Brass.

Light and texture, seeing and touching. How ingenious to tie it all together in the central image of the lens which the Pope holds in his hands!

Several of Bronzino's portraits of wealthy and powerful patrons are displayed in the Uffizi, and his figures sometimes have a stiff unreality like statues from Madame Tussaud's Wax Museum. Yet, in his *Lamentation for the Dead Christ*, Bronzino shows himself capable of portraying profound emotion with astonishing eloquence. His sensitive exploration of grief is conceived as a poem of hands and faces. Echoing the three crosses in the background on a distant hill, the three figures in the foreground suffer each in their own way.

There's a profound harmony between the two Marys, a sense of shared grief that is their common bond. Their communion is expressed in the way they look at Jesus, the turn of their bodies, the manner in which they reach out their hands to hold and touch the lifeless body. We can imagine that the older woman remembers the child who, almost a lifetime ago, would lie sleeping stretched out across her lap. For the younger woman we sense a different kind of anguish evoked in the simple gesture of touching her hand to her heart. The Madonna's head is covered, and she's dressed in muted colors of stiff cloth. Mary Magdalen's hair is unbound; her clothing is supple and radiant in vibrant colors of red, blue and gold. Maternal love and passionate love mourn their common loss.

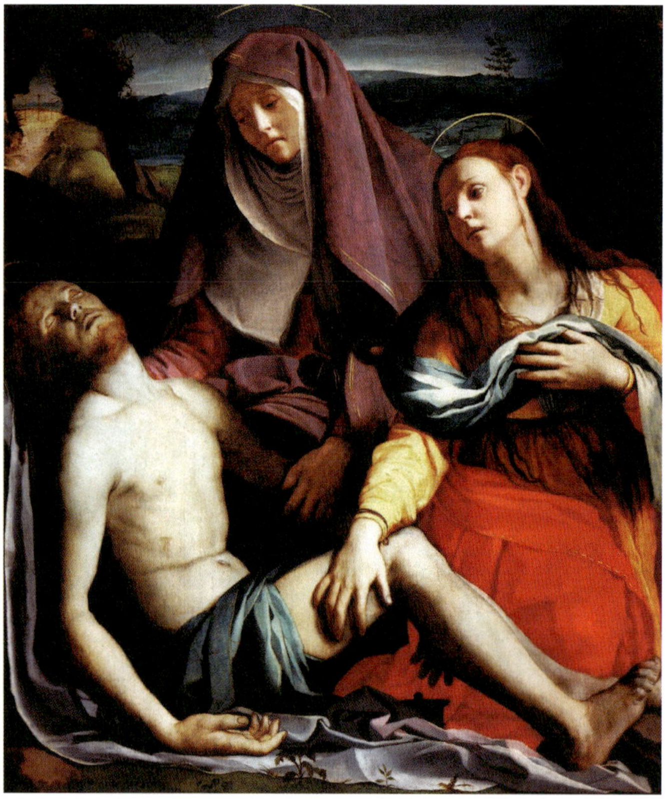

Figure 33: Bronzino's *Lamentation for the Dead Christ*

Christ's face, turned upward in utter surrender, echoes his palm. His fingers uncurl in the ease of death while Magdalen's remain intent, tense. Below and to the right of Christ's knees, on the far side of his body, we see the limp fingers of his left hand obscured in shadow as Magdalen's is bathed in light. The hands face each other across the expanse of the body as if they would reach across death to touch once more.

Let your eyes focus only on the lower right quadrant of the painting for just a moment. Look at the gold of Mary Magdalen's sleeve, the way her hand drapes across his thigh, the intense contrast between the burning red of her dress and the coolness of his flesh. At some point you'll notice Magdalen's jar of ointment, dark as a secret, nestled just beyond the folds of Christ's shroud. Its presence reminds us of the time when, before they were broken and bloodied, she lovingly bathed and rubbed his feet. His dangling fingers seem to reach for it as if toward a memory of bliss.

Beccafumi's Self-Portrait **Room 27**

Just to the left of Bronzino's *Lamentation for the Dead Christ* is a self-portrait of Domenico Beccafumi, probably the greatest Sienese artist of the 16th century. If by chance you are headed toward Siena after Florence, you'll see Beccafumi's work all throughout Siena's churches and museums. His *Fall of the Rebel Angels* in Siena's Pinacoteca gallery is an astonishing masterpiece. In any event, here's a chance to get acquainted.

Notice how the funny tuft of hair that sticks out from the front of his turban looks almost like a pair of horns, a bit like a demonic Moses.

Since first looking at his work, I've always had my suspicions that Beccafumi was profoundly unorthodox in his religious views. His self-portrait shows him to be of dark and brooding temperament, and he is clearly at pains to depict himself as no man's fool.

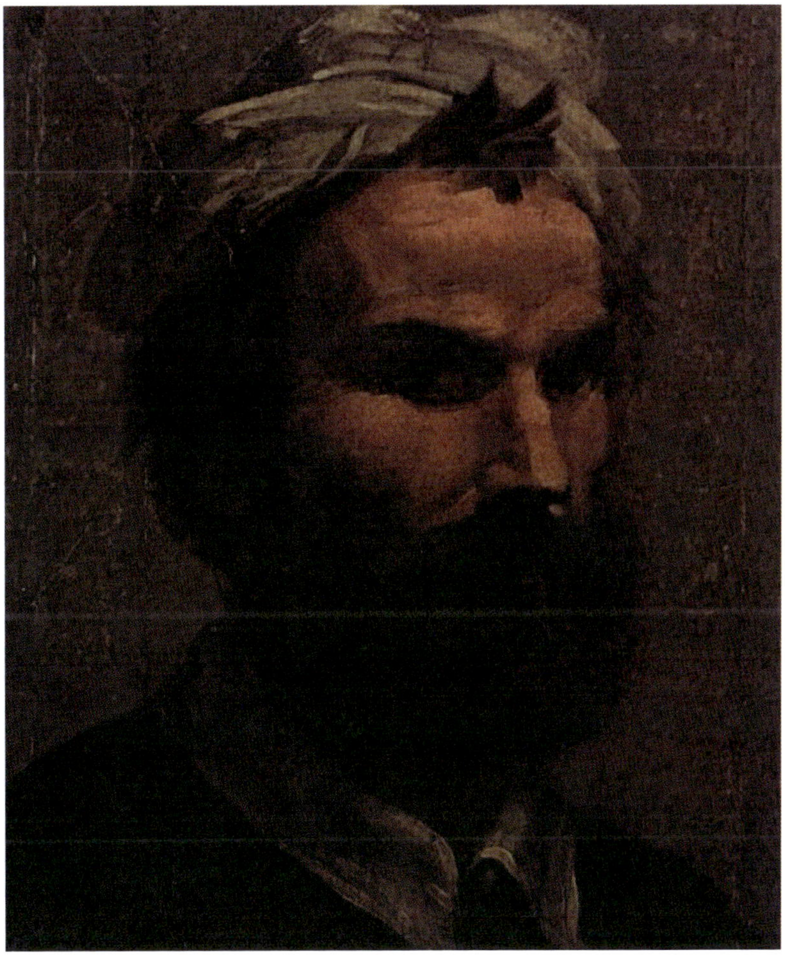

Figure 34: Beccafumi's *Self-Portrait*

A bit more about his work when we look next at Bronzino's *Pygmalion and Galatea.*

The myth of Pygmalion and Galatea is familiar to many people indirectly through the popular musical, *My Fair Lady*. In the modern version of the story, an erudite scholar educates and transforms an illiterate flower girl into a such paragon of grace and wit that he falls madly in love with her. In the ancient version, the artist Pygmalion carves a statue of such beauty that he falls in love with her, and he prays to Venus that she may come to life.

In this painting Bronzino shows us the moment when Pygmalion has dropped his hammer and chisels and kneels before the girl of his dreams with his hands clasped in prayer. He appears to have sacrificed a bull to Venus on her altar (you can just barely see the name of the Goddess on the curved plaque on the right side of the altar). Pygmalion stares intently at his beloved while Galatea looks out directly at us, somewhat bemused.

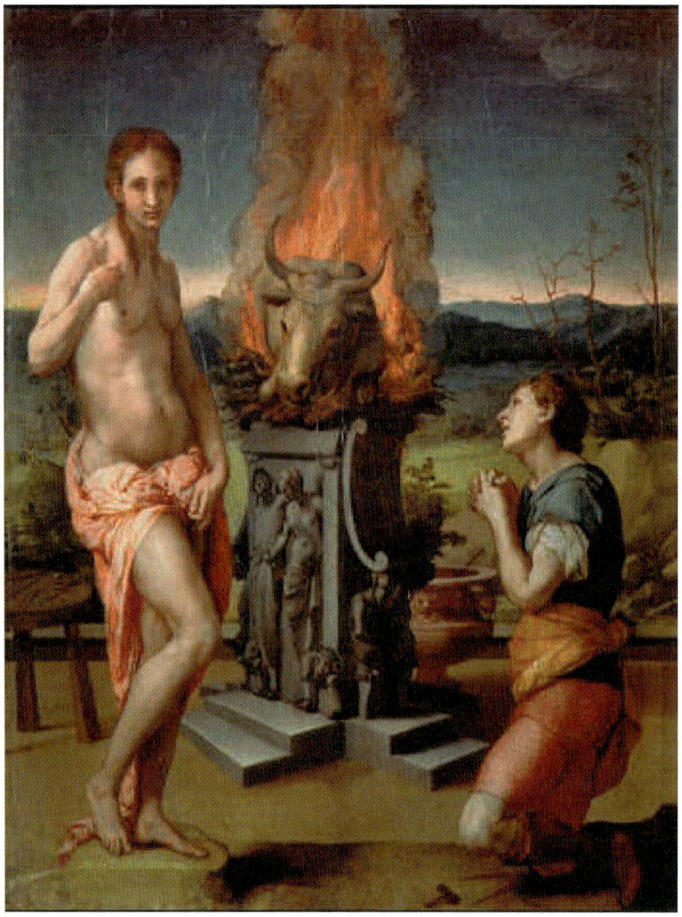

Figure 35: Bronzino's *Pygmalion and Galatea*

We may assume that Pygmalion is offering a sacrifice to Venus in the hope that she may grant his wish to have the statue before him come to life.

Yet, if you look at the bull, you'll find there's something curious about him. He seems distinctly unfazed by the fact that he is being sacrificed in flames on an altar. There's a look of quiet intelligence and composure in his face as he gazes at Galatea.

If you ever have the opportunity to visit the Siena Cathedral when its marble pavements are uncovered, you'll find a cycle of images by Domenico Beccafumi that invites comparison. It depicts the moment when the ancient Israelites create the Golden Calf while Moses is up on the mountain talking with God. As the High Priest Aaron tosses gold jewelry into the fire, the Golden Calf formed in the flames has the same unperturbed look and intelligent gaze as the bull in Bronzino's painting. In Beccafumi's treatment of this theme, there's little doubt that his sympathies lie with the peaceful celebrants who dance around the image and not with the righteous iconoclasts who murder them all. (This is, after all, not an unreasonable position for an artist to take, given that he spends all his days making those graven images which are explicitly forbidden by the Second Commandment.)

The ancient traditions of animating statues have largely disappeared from view in the modern world—with the notable exception of the story we all know about the wooden puppet whose nose grew longer every time he told a lie. Nevertheless, they were well known to the artistic intelligentsia of early 16th century Florence both from St. Augustine's writings, which denounced the practice, as well as from a body of esoteric writings, known as the *Corpus Hermeticum,* which praised it. (The translation and publication of the hermetic texts in the previous century had been sponsored by none less than Cosimo de' Medici himself.)

Bronzino's depiction of Pygmalion and Galatea stands in this tradition of tales about the animation of statues. In the figures that are sculpted around the sides of the altar, Bronzino plays with the boundary line between the animate and the inanimate, and with our own relationship to it. Look at the pair in the frieze on the left side of the altar: she hands him an apple, he puts his arm around her shoulders. What are they up to? Should we care? After all, they are just monopods, mere decorative elements whose bodies finish in a single limb. It's possible also that they each also have only one arm. Look at the figures on the right side of the altar that have only upper torsos. Then, go back to the other side of the altar, and look at the ram's heads at the base. Do you see how the one on the right is staring off to our right with a mischievous look on his face? Are these fragments mere decoration, or are we to understand that they alive? Are they as alive as Galatea? Is Galatea now as alive as Pygmalion?

But, wait a moment. It is just a painting after all, isn't it? Yes, and isn't it strange how we feel compelled to discriminate between the living and the dead in a wholly fictive universe? And isn't it even stranger that when we enter these worlds and dream them alive, we feel so much more alive ourselves?

***

There is another aspect to this painting which adds a light touch and gives us some sense of Bronzino's keen level of psychological insight and sense of humor. It has to do with the reason that artists always fall in love with their models, students with their teachers, and patients with their therapists. Jung described this phenomenon as "anima projection" and suggested that we each carry within us an image of the "ideal other" which we project upon a more or less suitable figure as circumstances permit. Freud described it in general terms as "transference" and specifically in erotic relationships as "the over-valuation of the love object."

There's a hint of all this is the way that Bronzino has rendered Pygmalion's dream girl. She's a bit lanky, has stringy hair, a rather large nose, modest breasts, and a hint of a double chin. Which is not to say that she is unattractive, only that she in no way conforms to the classical canons of feminine beauty. Is Bronzino slyly suggesting that, like many of his fellow artists and sculptors, Pygmalion thinks far too highly of his own work? Or is it just that every man always falls in love with the most beautiful girl in the world?

Titian's *Venus of Urbino* is based on an earlier painting by the Venetian artist, Giorgione, which shows Venus in a very similar pose against a natural landscape, sleeping or dreaming. Titian moves her indoors, opens her eyes, and has her gaze directly at the viewer.

Very much like Botticelli in his *Primavera* and *Birth of Venus*, Titian tries to evoke the experience of Aphrodite, not just tell about it. He invites us to enter the realm of Aphrodite which is, among other things, the realm of beauty and eros. As Sir Kenneth Clark insisted in his book on the history of the nude, to discuss such images in terms of compositional values while ignoring their erotic power is not an expression of superior morality but, rather, of simple dishonesty.

Part of the fascination of Titian's painting is the sphinx-like look with which Venus meets the viewer's own gaze. There is something about her look that captivates and entrances; we feel compelled to keep looking at her. Our eyes wander across the soft curves of her body, take in the background figures and furnishings, but keep returning to meet her gaze of erotic invitation.

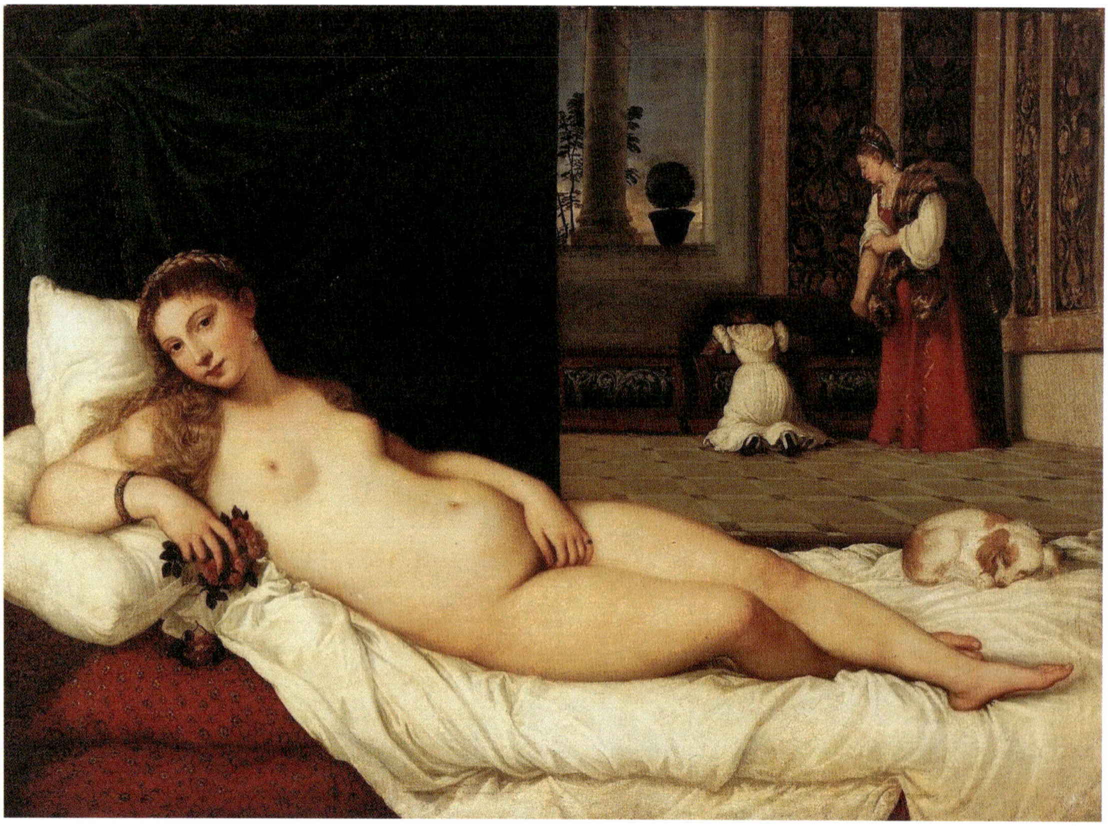

Figure 36: Titian's *Venus of Urbino*

In several of the contexts where female nakedness is depicted, in such encounters as David and Bathsheba, or Acteon and Diana, or Susanna and the Elders, there is a clear suggestion of voyeurism and of the invasiveness of the lustful male gaze. There is no hint of that in Titian's painting.

Aphrodite is nude by design, not caught unawares. Her braids, earrings, bracelet and ring are adornments that enhance the beauty of her naked body. Even her toenails glisten. She knows she's being admired and desired, and she basks in that very gaze as her birthright and reason-for-being. She is so perfectly at ease as she luxuriates on her couch of love with its rumpled sheet and its soft, plump pillows.

Like Botticelli before him, Titian suggests that Aphrodite stands (or lies) at the intersection of nature and culture. Look at how the sheet is pulled away to show us the fabric of the couch. In case we miss the point, Aphrodite has dropped one of nature's flowers onto the fabric's elegant pattern of abstract flowers. The tiny flowers are painted in gold and black, flowers of art that you will never find in nature. Aphrodite is the Goddess of both kinds of flowers, the force that harmonizes the world of made and the world of born.

Have you noticed how the painting is divided into two equal sections? On the left hangs a dark green curtain; on the right is a scene of domestic interiority. Cover your view of the right half of the painting for a moment with your hand or with a book. You'll find yourself alone in a private erotic encounter with the Goddess. Cover the left half of the painting, and you'll catch a glimpse of a woman lying in bed at home. We see a day in the life: the round of household chores, a domestic interior with wall hangings, chests of clothes and bedding, a potted plant and a lapdog.

Is it simple coincidence that the boundary line between these two realms runs right through the Mound of Venus? Or, are we to understand that the length of Aphrodite's body and her couch of love are what span and unite these two domains?

If you look carefully, you'll notice that the setting of the couch is somewhat lower than the floor plane of the room behind it. This suggests that our encounter takes place in a sort of antechamber to the room behind it. In other words: first comes love; then comes marriage; then it's time to make the beds and get on with the day.

***

Quite often, when you read about little dogs in Renaissance paintings, like this one curled up on the bed, you will be informed that the dog is a "symbol of marital fidelity". Here, however, I would suggest that the dog's role is to invite further reflection on the phenomena of domestication and domesticity.

Consider man's best friend: unable to dispatch their prey with a single blow like the great lion, dogs always hunted in packs. Biting, ripping and worrying their prey, they pursued it until it was weak with loss of blood and could finally be brought down and devoured as it lay dying. The domestication of these animals over the course of the centuries was no small feat. Neither is the taming of sexuality within marriage.

The raw power of sexuality, as we learn from the ancient stories of the Gods, was a nasty business. From Uranus to Philomela to Medea to Nestor, the classical myths tell tales of fatal attractions: lust, violence and rape; mutilation and castration; jealousy, vengeance and murder.

Aphrodite, however, was perceived during the Renaissance as a civilizing force. Born transmogrified from the severed genitals of Uranus, she invited sublimation of desire rather than simple repression. Through the transformative power of Beauty, she could turn the raging beast of urgent lusts and orgiastic hungers into a civilized being of planned trysts, erotic longing and voluptuous delays. The little dog curled up at Aphrodite's feet suggests that such things are at least possible. Behold Beauty and the Beast.

***

Parting thought: there's no doubt but that Titian understood very well the primitive savagery of wild eros. In the various paintings he did of Bacchus and of his worshippers, he conjures some of Western man's most vivid images of these powerful forces. In Titian's painting of the meeting of Bacchus and Ariadne which hangs in the National Gallery in London (Figure 37) , the little dog appears once again. Ariadne's pet with his cute collar confronts a pagan goat-boy who drags along the head of a stag that the revelers have recently dismembered. Fido barks at the goat-boy who doesn't even know he's there. We are further than most of us dare to imagine from domestic interiors and marital fidelity.

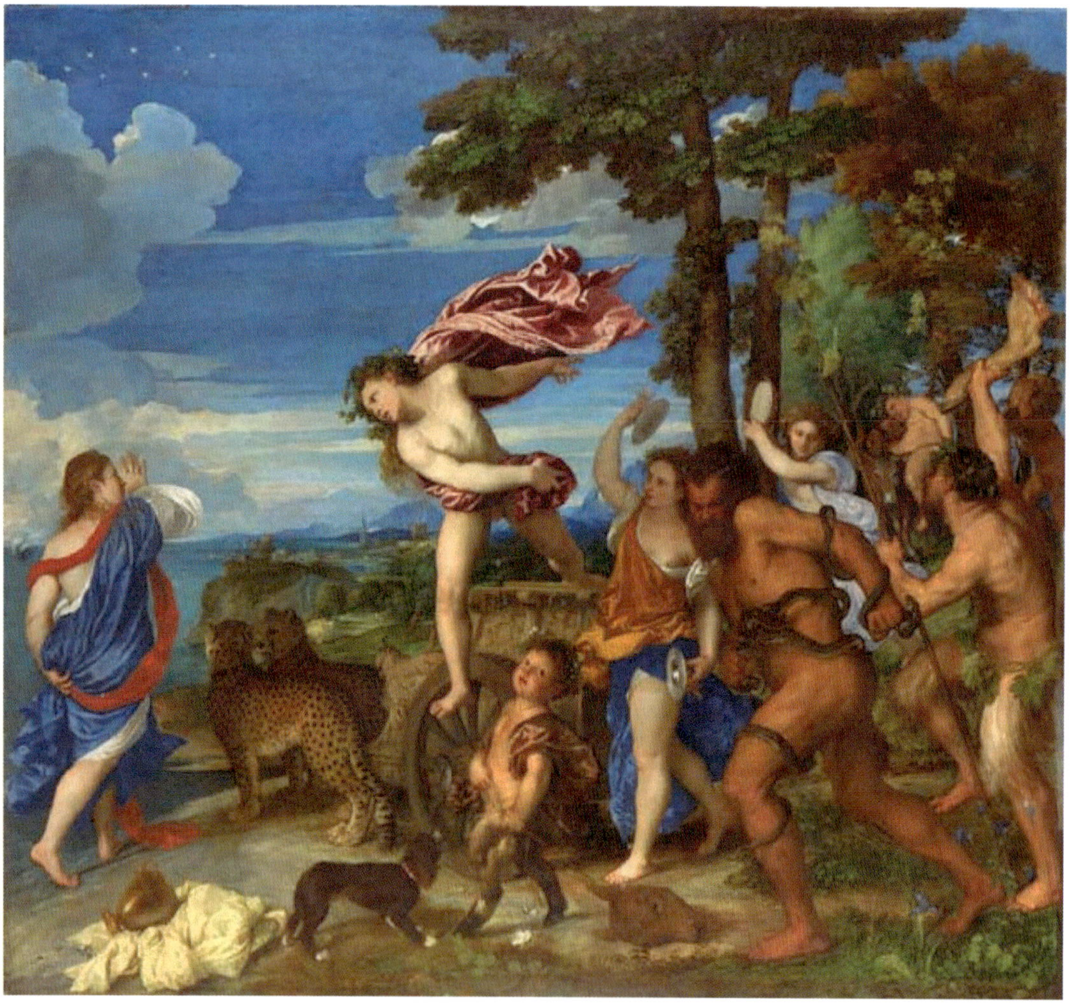

Figure 37: Titian's *Bacchus and Ariadne*

Titian's *Flora* **Room 28**

Flora is the Latin word for "flower." Flora is also the name of the Roman Goddess who was generally depicted striding forward and broadcasting flowers. There is a statue of Flora along the corridor of the upper floor of the Uffizi that you may have noticed; you might also remember her as the second female figure from the right in Botticelli's *Primavera*.

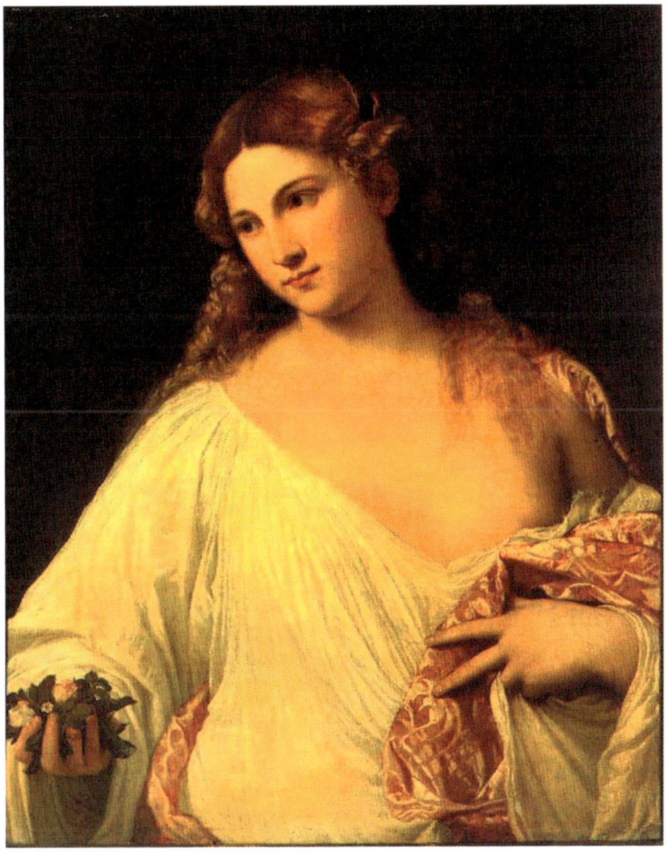

Figure 38: Titian's *Flora*

Titian shows us Flora as a young woman who is flowering. Whereas Titian's Venus holds her flowers as fact, as an attribute of her beauty, Flora holds hers in offering. Like the invitation of her partially bared breast, she extends her flowers as a token of her readiness for love.

The feathery delicacy of her hair as it falls on her bare shoulder is part of the erotic beauty of this image. As is the way that her breast is bared to show just a hint of her nipple. From the erotic interplay of what is seen and what is left to be imagined, she weaves her spell.

***

Titian is the last great master of the Italian Renaissance whose work I find thoroughly satisfying. Although there are many other talented artists who continue to paint over the course of the century, none of them has the greatness of soul and depth of understanding, combined with artistic brilliance, that Titian embodies.

If you have made it this far, your cup is probably filled to overflowing, and your feet are probably killing you. So, from this point forward, the remaining notes are offered in the hope of bringing a few interesting works to your attention as you make your way slowly toward the exit.

Room 29 includes a pair of striking images by Parmigianino, known as the *Saint Zachariah Madonna* and *The Madonna of the Long Neck.* Both are exemplary works in the style of painting known as "Mannerism" of which Parmigianino was a leading exponent. Just as Michelangelo had done with his statues, Mannerist painting occasionally distorted the human figure in order to enhance beauty or expressiveness—often at the cost of plausibility or verisimilitude.

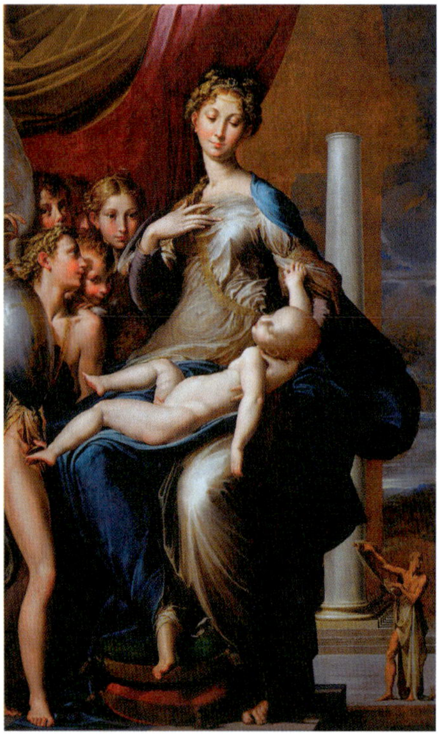

Figure 39: Parmigianino's *Madonna of the Long Neck*

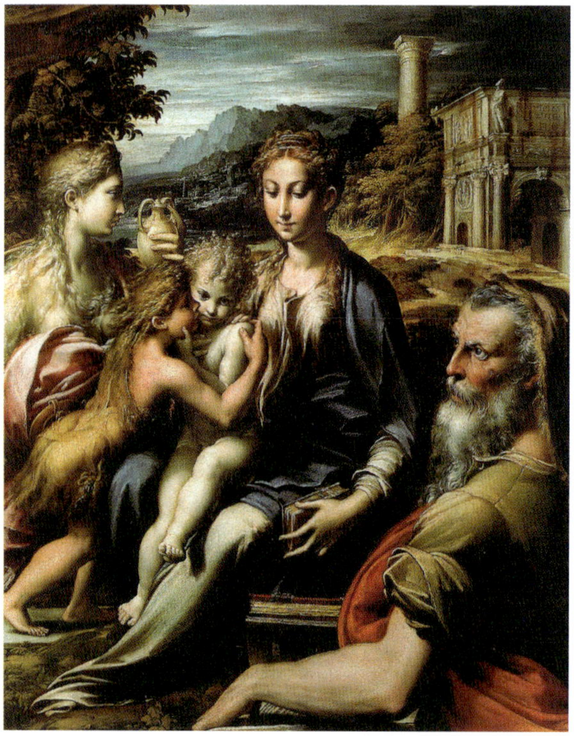

Figure 40: Parmigianino's *St. Zacchariah Madonna*

Mannerism was despised for centuries as an expression of decadence after the great flowering of the High Renaissance. Later it was "rehabilitated" as the legitimate expression of a society tormented by conflict and change. I prefer to think of Mannerism as an experimental, exploratory movement by artists who were looking for new things to do after Raphael had already achieved perfection in other channels. Some of these experiments were exciting and successful; others were not.

Parmigianino seems to be exploring a strange sort of merger of the classical and Christian worlds. In each of these paintings, the Holy Family is depicted in a mysterious pagan realm of columns and temples. But unlike some of the other paintings we've seen, the pagan world is evoked here as the very context of the story, rather than as an element to provide contrast. The movement and depiction of these Christian figures are based on classical prototypes. In the *Saint Zachariah Madonna*, Mary Magdalen appears in sharp profile as a nude maenad, while the young John the Baptist has the shapely, accentuated buttocks of a Cupid. He aggressively embraces Jesus who shies away from him like a reluctant lover. In both paintings we're invited, possibly for the first time, to admire the Madonna's firm round breasts with their erect nipples poking the fabric of her dress.

Daring and inventive, definitely. Meaningful? We're left wondering...

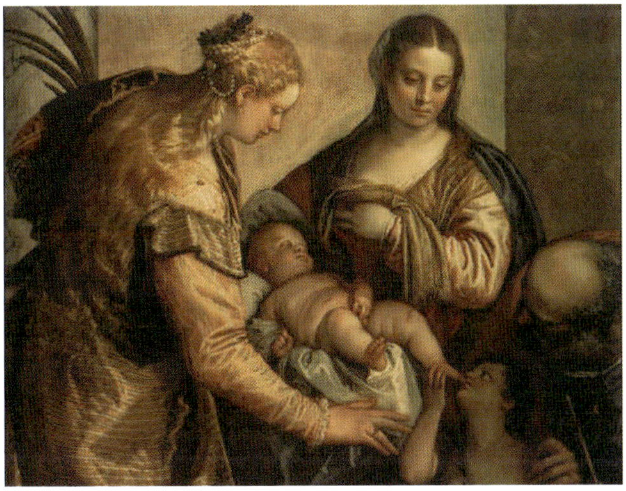

Figure 41: Veronese's
Holy Family with Saint Catherine

After 250 years of exquisite depictions of fabric in Italian painting, it's hard to imagine that anyone could come along and do something new. Yet, Veronese renders the colors and textures of cloth in ways that were unprecedented and remain breathtakingly beautiful.

Look at the way the light plays off the folds of St. Catherine's dress, and off the sleeve of her outstretched arm. The interplay of light between the fabric of her dress and the tresses of her golden hair as it cascades down her back is especially lovely.

Meanwhile, I have to admit that every time I look at the martyrdom of St. Justine, I find myself unable to care very much about what's taking place, despite my best efforts to find some pathos or drama in this scene. In general, I try to enjoy Veronese for the beauty of his colors and surfaces without looking too much for depth or sincerity.

Nevertheless, I find myself appalled and incredulous that anyone could murder a woman who is so beautifully dressed. The reddish-silver sheen and luster of her gown is simply dazzling...

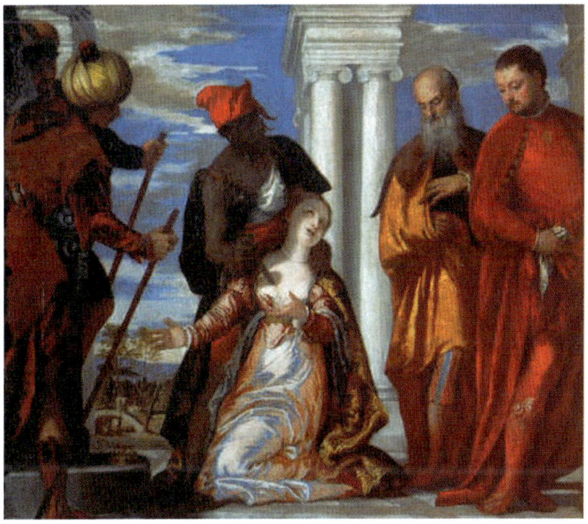

Figure 42: Veronese's *Martyrdom of St. Justine*

Room 33 is long narrow room, known as "The Corridor of the 16th Century," which contains a miscellany of smaller paintings. Fourth on your left as you enter the room is a painting by Duke Cosimo's court painter, Vasari, known as *Vulcan's Forge*.

In a dimly lit cavernous hall we catch a glimpse of Vulcan's underworldly realm of fire, hammering and forceful activity. The Goddess Minerva has stopped by to inform Vulcan of his deliverables. As one of the *putti* holds her spear, she displays the latest project requirements in front of Vulcan's face.

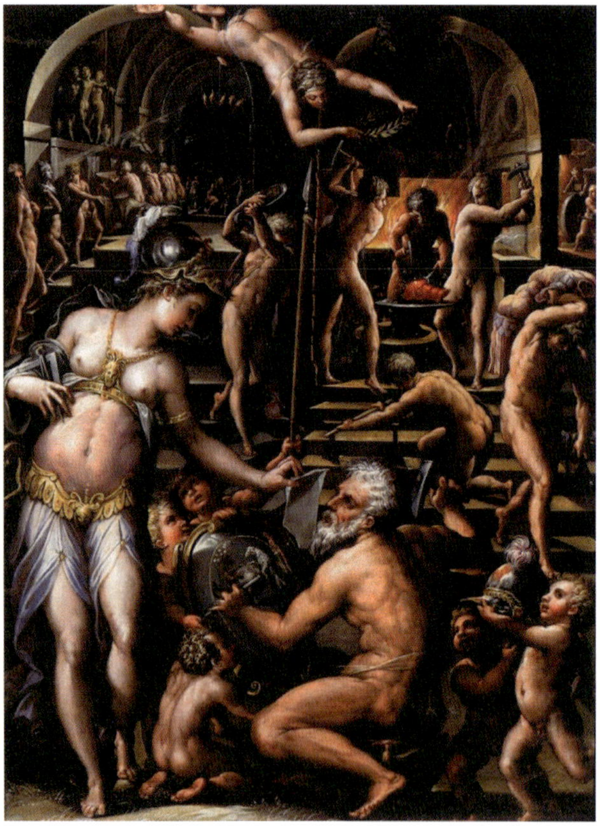

Figure 43: Vasari's *Forge of Vulcan*

If you've ever worked in the product development arena in the corporate world, you may recognize Minerva as the Goddess of Project Management. (Our English word, "project," comes from the Latin "iecto, iectus," meaning, "to throw a spear.") Unlike sustaining activities such as planting or weaving, a project is a one-time effort to achieve a specific goal, fraught with risk, much like throwing a spear at a moving target.) Minerva appears here as a representative of management letting Vulcan know what's needed and by when. The head of Medusa, which Minerva wears on her breast, has the power to turn living things into stone. (If you don't believe in such things, try reading sometime the Project Management Institute's *Guide to the Project Management Body of Knowledge* whose power of reification is rivaled only by the State Penal Code.) In the distance, up on the left, you can see the artists seated at their workstations focusing diligently as they try to meet their deadlines.

Grand Duke Cosimo I and, later, his son, Francesco, established the modern world's first product development teams, with budgets dedicated to supporting sustained research in working environments not unlike the one shown here. Cosimo's first R&D project was to rediscover a way to cut the hard, reddish stone known as "porphyry." The ability to harden chisels sufficiently to cut porphyry was a process well known to the ancients but lost somehow in the interim. To this end Cosimo funded several smithing workshops that worked continuously to find ways to harden metal tools sufficiently to once again cut porphyry. Much to their credit, they eventually succeeded. And, to proclaim and publicize this impressive achievement, Duke Cosimo commissioned a statue of Justice to be carved entirely out of porphyry. You can still see it displayed on top of the column which stands in Florence's Piazza Trinità along the via Tornabuoni.

Cosimo's son and heir, Francesco, continued to fund research and development teams and can be credited with bringing to market the first reasonable facsimile of fine white porcelain to be developed outside the Orient. This story of Duke Cosimo I and his quest to cut porphyry, as well as a thousand other fascinating insights and observations, may be found in Joscelyn Godwin's *The Pagan Dream of the Renaissance* (Grand Rapids: Phanes Press, 2002), certainly the most interesting book on this period that you are likely to find.

Jacopo Zucchi's *The Golden Age* **Room 33**

Further along the same wall on your left, you'll find Jacopo Zucchi's lovely rendering of *The Age of Gold*, the mythical Golden Age when all was bliss before we started on our downhill slide. The Age of Gold is regularly described as the pagan equivalent of the Garden of Eden. But, to be fair, it looks like there was much more of a community and that they had a far richer sense of how to have fun once they were done with naming the animals.

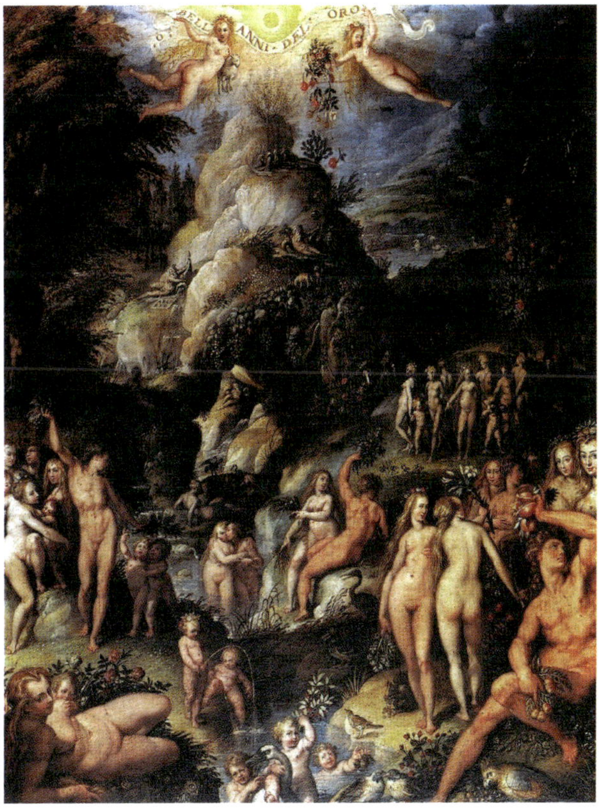

Figure 44: Jacopo Zucchi's *The Golden Age*

Fruit, flowers, erotic embraces, swans, nudity, nursing babies, skinny dipping, dancing, sunshine and bodily innocence. If you are old enough to remember Be-Ins, Woodstock, and the Summer of Love, you will recognize many of these familiar elements that seem to reappear whenever the perennial dream of heaven-on-earth erupts in the human imagination. (Although, quite honestly, I don't remember the swans...)

When you are ready to move on, make your way back to the main corridor and turn left, walking toward the museum cafeteria. There's one last set of paintings that would be a shame to miss before heading back down the stairs. You'll find them in Room 44.

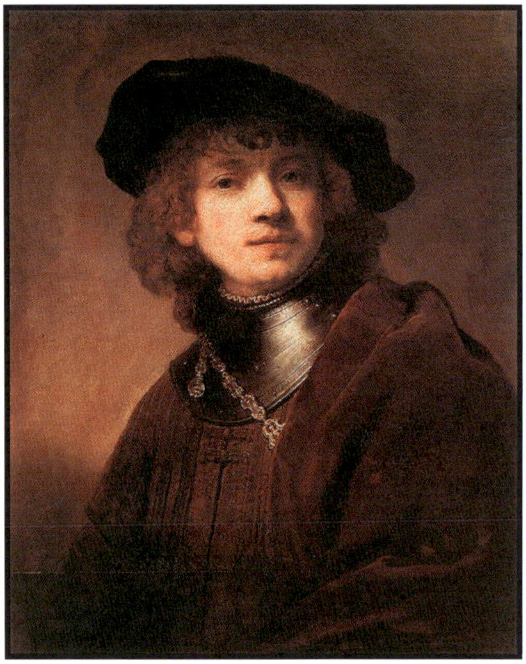

Figure 45: Rembrandt's Self-Portrait As a Young Man

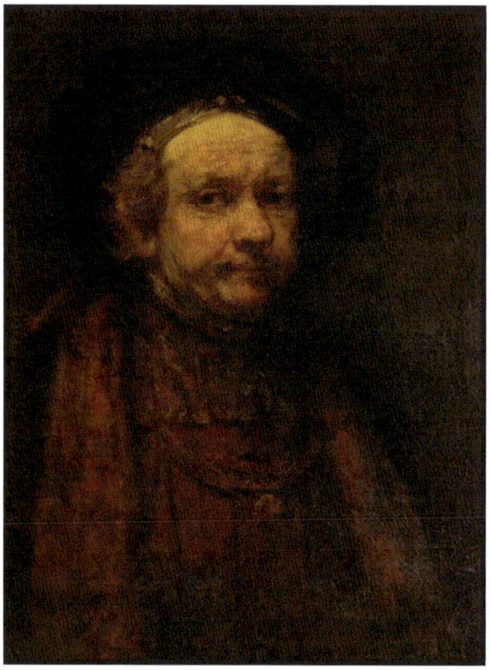

Figure 46: Rembrandt's Self-Portrait As an Old Man

On either side of Rembrandt's painting of an elderly Rabbi hang two of the many self-portraits he did over the course of his lifetime. The one on the left shows him as a handsome young man, elegantly dressed in hat and coat with a stylish collar. He looks out toward us as if looking toward the future itself, with honesty and vulnerability and a certain measure of courage and confidence.

In the portrait on the right, we see him toward the end of his years. All the flattery and all the specific detail of the earlier portrait are gone. All that is left is a look.

We may think of Rembrandt as one of the world's great painters, but the old man who looks at himself takes little comfort in all that. He knows about all that he once dreamt of doing and how little of it ever saw the light of day, how much of it was done poorly, how differently it all turned out. He's old now; the game is almost over.

Nowadays, our friends would come over and tell us we're being too hard on ourselves. Lighten up, look at all the things you have to be thankful for. Have you thought about antidepressants?

It's understandable when they cheer us on in this way. When we see a man take his own measure with such ruthless honesty, it's more than most of us can bear.

***

I try to visit with Rembrandt's young and old selves every time I come to the Uffizi, often as the last thing I do before leaving. I do a certain exercise once suggested to me by my friend, Nils Peterson. I imagine the young self I once was, looking out at the grown man who now stands before him. And I ask: Of all the young man's dreams, what is it that most needs to be honored at this time of life?

Then I turn to the old man, who always breaks my heart, and ask what I will regret most bitterly when my time comes. Then I go on my way.

Afterward

My intention in writing the ***The Uffizi Gallery*** was to provide a guidebook that could serve as a virtual companion for your armchair travels as well as a hands-on guidebook for your on-site visits to Tuscany.

My wife, Pam Mercer, and I have been leading tours in Tuscany and in other parts of Europe for nearly fifteen years. We have learned from working with groups that energy and attention have their limits, so rather than trying to cover everything, we focus only on what's most interesting. We try to approach art and cultural history as something that belongs to all of us. We love sharing our passion for art with travelers who are not academic specialists, but who are looking for something more satisfying than the conventional patter of travel guides and canned recitations.

Join Us in Italy!

If you would like to join us on one of our cultural travel adventures, have a look at the full listing of our scheduled offerings for this season on our website at: http://www.tuscanytours.com/

Be prepared for an immersion in the local culture that includes exquisite hotels, visits to extraordinary places, stimulating presentations and lively conversation, and some of the finest food and wine you'll find anywhere on the planet!

Free Newsletter: Art and Life in Tuscany

And, if you'd like to keep in touch with Tuscany throughout the year, sign up to receive our free periodic newsletter and read our blog. You'll find insights and observations about Tuscan life, Italy travel, food, wine and culture. Find more information at our website at: http://www.tuscanytours.com/

6117050R00041

Printed in Great Britain
by Amazon.co.uk, Ltd.,
Marston Gate.